Value-Oriented Education

Value-Orinted Education in Schools

Theory and Practice

Prof. Rajinder M. Kalra

SHIPRA

Rs. 200/-
SHIPRA

ISBN: 978-81-7541-158-6

2014 Impression
(2009, 2006, 2004, 2001)

Value-Oriented Education in Schools

Published by:
SHIPRA PUBLICATIONS
H.O.: LG 18-19, Pankaj Central Market, I.P. Ext.,
Patparganj, Delhi 110092, Ph. 22235152, 22236152
Br. Off.: 4617/18, Main Ansari Road, Daryaganj,
New Delhi 110002; Ph.9650028065, 9810522367
Email: info@shiprapublications.com
Website: www.shiprapublications.com

To

My grand daughters

Shreya and Ayushi Uppal

with love

Value Education is
Exploration not imposition

There are certain things that our age needs, and certain things that it should avoid. It needs compassion and a wish that mankind should be happy; it needs a desire for knowledge and the determination to eschew pleasant myths; it needs above all courageous hope and impulse to creativeness. The things that it must avoid are cruelty, envy, greed, competitiveness, search for irrational subjective certainty, and what Freudians called the death wish.... The root of the matter is very simple and old fashioned thing.... The Thing I mean, please forgive me for mentioning it—is love, Christian love or compassion. If you feel this, you have a motive for existence, a guide in action, a reason for courage, an imperative society for intellectual necessity.

Bertrand Russel
Study of Science & Its Impact on Society

Preface

UNESCO organized a "Values in Education" Summit in 1998, to encourage schools to review their curricula in terms of value education. The fact that a world body like UNESCO should stress on the need of teaching 'values' in the school system is in itself a statement of the gravity of the problems created by gradual disappearance of such virtues and morals that are essential for maintenance of a civil society and the preservation of democracy.

Until recently both parents and schools shared the responsibility of shaping the character of the young without much debate because religion, tradition and society in general had clear cut definitions of the moral and immoral, right and wrong, and good and bad. But with the advent of science and technology, universalization of education, the industrial revolution, the pragmatism born out of the necessity to survive in the competitive world, the old ways, the morals and the very definition of virtues underwent a metamorphosis. In the resulting confusion of heterogeneous society, the educational institutions as well as parents have become increasingly unsure about their contributions in transmitting the values that would be relevant in the changing modern society. But before we can arrive at any conclusion about teaching of values in the schools it would be quite relevant to define the word 'Values'.

The word 'Values' was first used by the German Philosopher Friedrich Nietzsche in 1880. Until then the word value was used as a verb meaning to value as esteem something or as a singular noun meaning the measure of something for example, the value of money, property or labour. Nietzsche used the word 'Values' in plural to denote moral beliefs and attitudes that were personal and subjective because he believed in what Darwin's "Origin of Species" taught him about the survival of the fittest. He, along with many other philosophers of his time, believed that 'virtues' and 'vices' 'good' and 'evil', as religions had been preaching, were not necessarily conducive for building strong persons. Compassion, humility and fear were of no value for a brave warrior. In the modern democratic society, this concept of values has changed. The word 'values' has come to be used in plurals for over a century. Thus, the universal values like Truth, Honesty, Compassion, Responsibility, Goodness, Beauty, Charity, Equality and Justice cannot be replaced by any subjective values.

In democratic societies, inculcating these values is imperative for maintaining law and order. For building good character of citizens, it is the responsibility of the educational institutes and the family to help young children to perceive the 'value' of such traits.

Building good character of young involves :

(a) developing the ability to judge what is right;

(b) to respect what is right;

(c) to help them become courageous to do the right.

We must realize that knowing what is good is not enough without desiring to do what is good and habitually doing what we believe to be right.

Thus, teaching objective values in schools, and guiding the young ones to make sense of their beliefs and values, needs to be taken very seriously by schools. The restoration of desirable character traits along with good manners can be possible only if family and community cooperate with educational institutions. In the shrinking global parameters, the need to inculcate objective or universal values is very urgent. Unless our children perceive themselves as the citizens of one world, peace, harmony and fraternity will gradually become just hollow words. Therefore, teachers, educators, and statesmen should strive for 'Value' based education in action in our school system.

Rajinder M. Kalra

Acknowledgements

The author is grateful to the following educationists for their inspiration and guidance in this humble academic venture concering value oriented education in the educational system.

- Prof. Kireet Joshi, Chairman, Indian Council of Philosophical Research (ICPR), Ministry of Human Resource Development.
- Prof. D.P. Chattopadhya, Chairman, Centre for Studies in specialization.
- Prof. N.K. Ambasht, Chairman and Dr. Kuldeep Agarwal, Director (Academic) of National Open School.

My special thanks and gratitude to Dr. J.D. Sharma, former Reader, NCERT and Senior Executive Officer, National Open School for his academic contributions in the finalisation of the manuscript especially in the chapter titled—Human Values in Education; Certain Practical Strategies and Mr. J.C. Aggarwal, Educationist, for contributing chapter on 'Human Rights Education.'

Rajinder M. Kalra

Acknowledgements

The author is grateful to the following educationists for their inspiration and guidance in this innovative endeavour concerning value oriented education in the Educational system.

- Prof. Kireet Joshi, Chairman, Indian Council of Philosophical Research (ICPR), Ministry of Human Resource Development.
- Prof. D.P. Chattopadhyaya, Chairman, Centre for Studies in Civilization.
- Prof. M.S. [illegible], Chairman and Dr. Kuldeep Agarwal, Director (Academic) of National Open School.

My special thanks and gratitude to Dr. J.S. Rajput, former Director, NCERT and former Executive Officer, National Open School for his academic contributions in the finalisation of the manuscript especially the chapter titled – Human Values in Education: Ancient Vision and Modern Strategies and Mr. J.C. Agarwal, Educationist, for contributing chapter on Value in Higher Education.

Rajinder M. Kalra

Contents

I

Inculcation of Human Values in the School System

(An Overview)

In ancient societies religion was the ruling force in every sphere of human life. Education was primarily value oriented based on religious dictums. Today when secularism is expected to be the basic ideology of all progressive democratic countries, the task of providing moral education without any reference to a particular religion is a challenge for the educators. At the same time there is the need at present for inculcation of values because of diminishing influence of religion, absence of elders in the nuclear family and individualism resulting in an unprecedented erosion in the values of the younger generation.

Concept of Values

The dictionary meaning of the term value is something that has worth, utility and importance. From a historical view point, a value may be defined as a thing which is good. Operationally, the concept of values may be defined as "factors which affect human behaviour".

Intellectually, value may be defined as a "concept which is accepted by the sub-conscious mind, is understood by all and perceived by the individual."

When we talk of human values, we generally refer to factors which affect human behaviour and emotional attitude. Thus, human behaviour is guided by values. The self centred individual of today puts personal gain (in monetary terms) as a single guiding value in his life and which can be detrimental for the society. Therefore, when we are striving for inculcating human values in education, our aim is to outline and manifest those values which would bring happiness to the individual and would be beneficial for the society and mankind as well.

Catagories of Values

Values may be categorized as follows:

(1) Essential values—These involve the basic nature of man himself.

(2) Personal values—What is profitable and good for the individual.

(3) Social values—What is good for the society. It discusses the basis of the relationship of the individual with other people.

(4) Cultural values—Which involve the survival of the culture.

(5) Institutional values—Which include the political values, the moral values and establishment values.

Other questions arise :

(i) Do the values themselves change?

(ii) Is it only our interpretation of constant values that change?

One can assume, that abstract values such as tolerance, self-respect, love, truth and patriotism remain constant. However, world events may bring about changes in priorities. During the Vietnam War, in the U.S.A., Draft dodging was considered by many as a sign of patriotism in comparison to going to war.

Furthermore, our rapidly changing society results in a constant reassessment of our values. Science, once regarded as wholly beneficial, has undergone a subtle value change in recent years. With its ramifications affecting the social, educational and political issues of our time, science has acquired an un-savoury characterization. The fact that we have the technical know-how to destroy the world, whether quickly through atomic war or slowly through pollution and environmental abuse, does not improve science's image. But we have not developed human values which may control the above destruction. Thus, we feel threatened.

However, there is a great danger in regarding science as a singular value system. If the weakness of various ethnic cultures is their resistance to scientific thinking, then there has been equal stubborness on the part of western scientific culture to be over-committed to technology. The historical records of all great civilizations show that cultural idealism and technology must exist side by side.

The great engineering master pieces in all ethnic cultures testify that science and technology are thousands of years old.

What Westerners call the "industrial revolution" was in reality only an unprecedented acceleration and exceedingly strong emphasis on a particular aspect of human activity.

The rise of the great civilizations was not brought about by technology alone, but by radically new social inventions.

Evidently both our society and its values are rapidly changing. Modern youth questions the values of their parents. If we are to cope with these changing attitudes, it is imperative to discuss the importance of values in our school system.

But, there is no need to Preach and Teach values to the youngsters. Once they understand these basic values, the relevance of these will be self evident. The child has learnt to appreciate all that truthful, beautiful and good and discard things and behaviour which are undesirable.

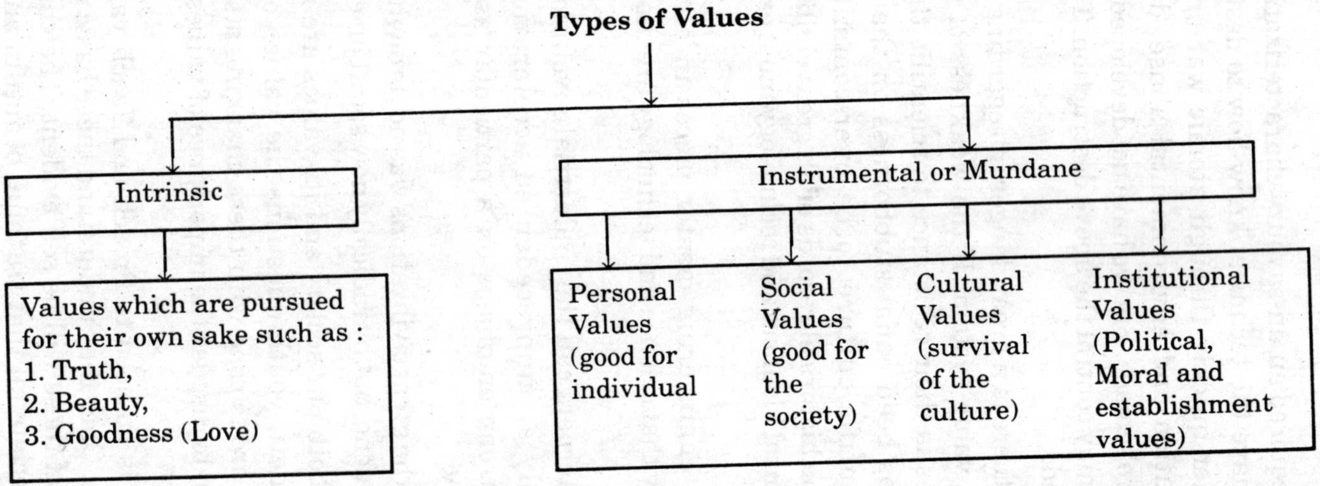
Types of Values
Intrinsic
Values which are pursued for their own sake such as :
1. Truth,
2. Beauty,
3. Goodness (Love)
Instrumental or Mundane
Personal Values (good for individual
Social Values (good for the society)
Cultural Values (survival of the culture)
Institutional Values (Political, Moral and establishment values)

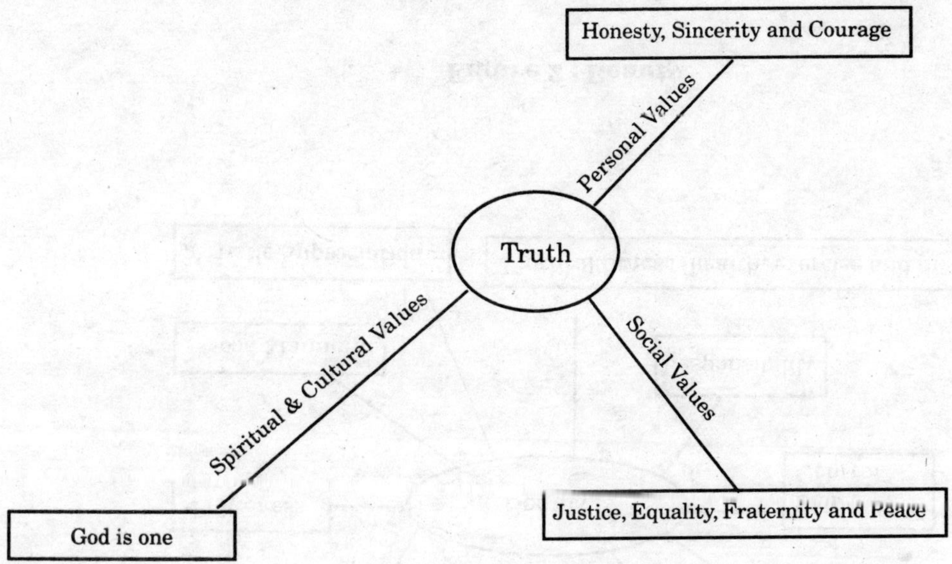

Figure 1 : Truth

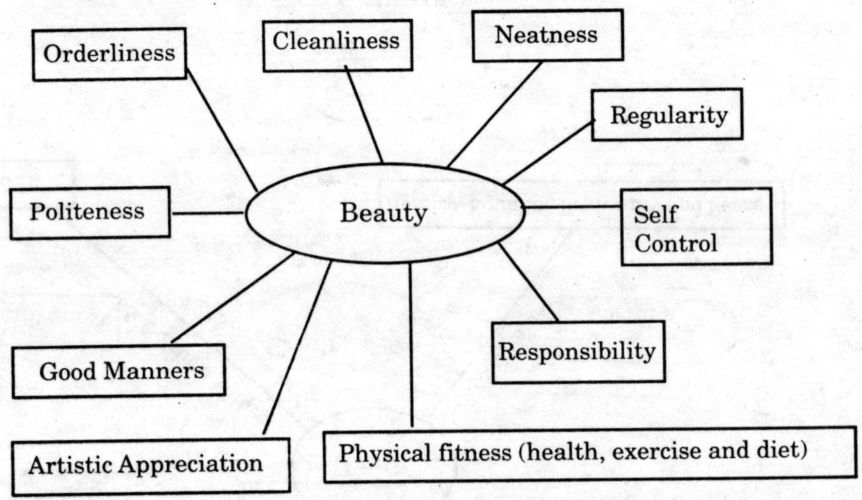

Figure 2 : Beauty

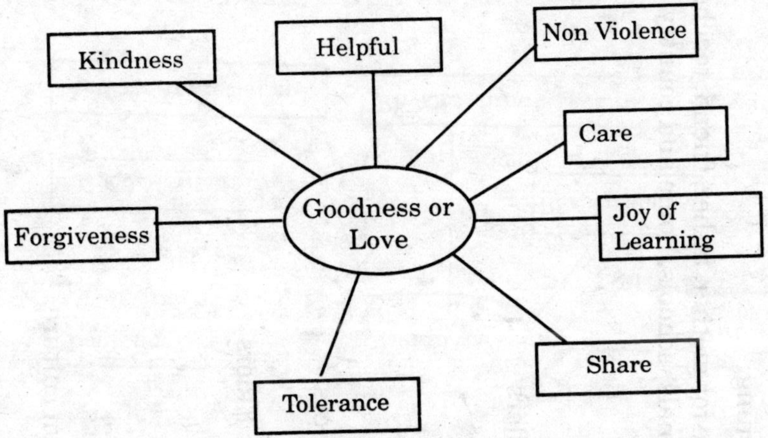

Figure 3 : Goodness or Love

Values in the School System

Different sets of values are to be encouraged/inculcated at different stages of school education.

Values at the Primary Level : The list of Values is as under —

Joy of Learning

Love – Love for mother, father, friend, teacher, nature, animals, schools, home and country.

Care

Share

Co-operate

Helping others

Forgiveness

Obedience

Cleanliness

Orderliness

Good Manners

Politeness

Respect for Elders

Kindness

Honesty

Courage

Fearlessness

Pride in own culture

Strategies for Inculcation of Values at Primary Level: Following strategies should be adopted —

- Exemplary behaviour of the teacher
- Demonstrating good manners, respect for elders and discipline (School and Home)
- Prayer (Meaning of the Prayer)

- Celebration of special days and festivals relating to different religions, national and international days
- Charts and pictures in the class
- Frequent meeting with parents

Values at the Secondary Level : These are as under—

1. Knowledge
2. Scientific Temper
3. International understanding
4. Spiritual Strength
5. Patriotism
6. Justice
7. Sincerity
8. Honesty
9. Courage
10. Respect for all religions
11. Patience
12. Good conduct
13. Tolerance
14. Broadness of vision, intuition
15. Development of grace, beauty, strength, and beauty of the soul and mind.

Character Formation and Assessment of Values

Today the youngsters are in "Values Crisis". Whether to accept "Western Values" in toto or 'rejection of traditional values' is a "crisis" issue.

Values are acquired by examples and these values are transmitted (caught) by what we do, not what we say to do. Teachers may be oriented with different strategies for assessing values.

1. *My Favourite Activities*
   Helping the student to examine his favourite activities, e.g., writing down fifteen things you like to do.

2. *Discouraging Apathy*
   To develop stronger and clearer point of view. Describing views about important issues like poverty and corruption.

3. *Comparing Values*
   To give a chance to see how others value things.

4. *Rating Values*
   Making decision of different degrees. Publicly stating his views and defending them.

5. *Where do you stand?*
   To determine strength of your feelings on certain values. Have a ladder of series of steps drawn in their notebooks.

6. *I am Proud*
   To build self confidence in the student. Your pride in relation to certain aspects of life.

7. *In the Public Eye*
   To give a person the chance to state his views in the classroom.

8. *Sharing Experience*
   To get to know each other by interviews in a small group.

9. *Learning to Listen*
   Every one has a right to express their own values.

10. *What are the Consequences*
    To search for consequences.

11. *Slicing the Apple of your Life*
    How do you spend your time and money? Draw a circle on your paper and divide it into four quarters depicting the life style.

12. *Make a Wish*
    To make you think about your value.
13. *What Am I?*
    To know yourself better. To think about your life objectively.
14. *Chapters of My Life.*
    To see your life as a whole to think of goals-past, present and future.
15. *Strength of Beliefs*
    To assess how strongly you believe in something.
16. *Picture of My Life*
    To think about where my life is going.

Teachers face an increasing number of curriculum decisions. An avalanche of knowledge in all academic areas, especially the sciences, has thundered upon man in the last twenty years.

How can teachers supply meaningful educational experiences for children in the light of this explosion in knowledge? Can teachers change the content of teaching in order to better meet the needs of their students, their communities, and their society? That this is a difficult, if not an impossible task for teachers to accomplish, is abundantly clear.

Furthermore, recent educational innovations have overlooked human growth. Instead of using modern "jargon" (such as programmed instruction, differentiated staffing, individualized learning and behavioural objectives), our emphasis should be on child growth and development. Human growth is directly related to the "Values" development among the children.

Students in developing countries are in the midst of an overwhelming "values" crisis. Seeking more of what western technology and culture can produce, some of the

Human Universal Values

(Truth, Beauty and Goodness as Root Values)

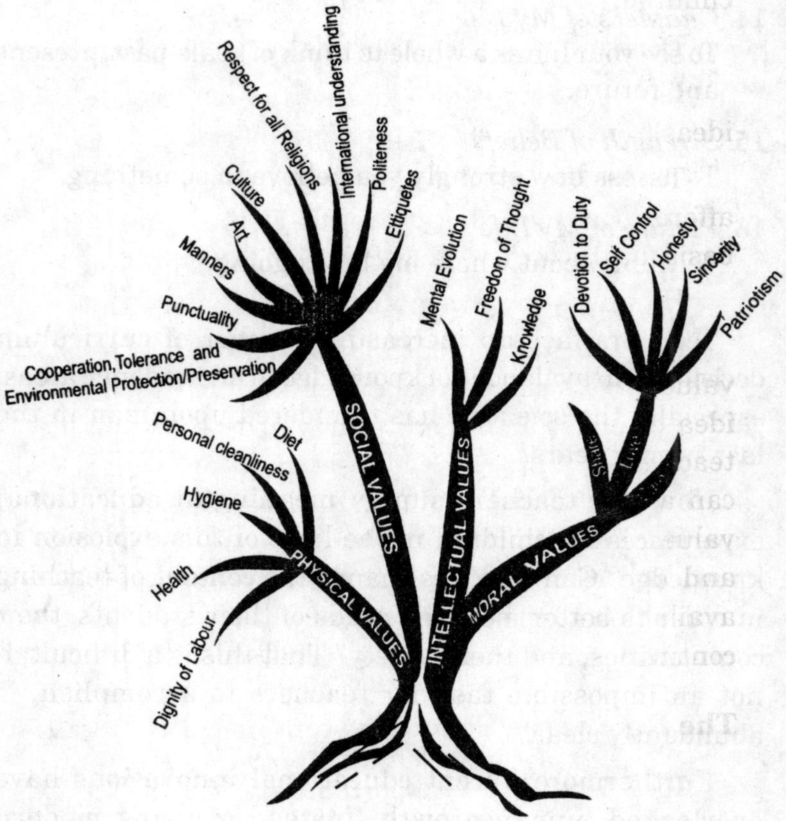

Figure 4 : Value Tree

students push for adoption of western ideas and practices. They are faced with a choice; either staying as they are or adopting the western value system in total and rejecting everything they have known. This confusion and conflict results in literally tearing apart the cultures of the children.

Does it have to be either choice?

Isn't it possible for children to amalgamate the best ideas from their own culture and that of the West's?

Teachers must provide a learning environment which affords both experiences desired by the child as well as a basis for the formal education goals of the schools.

How does one accomplish this task?

A promising approach for dealing with the emerging values crisis among the students is the rejection of the idea of imposing "right" values upon them. Instead we teach them a process and a set of criteria by which they can arrive at and evaluate the soundness of their own values. This approach might give students a set of tools and skills for sorting out the alternatives which are available and the consequences which may result as they continue to live with a focus on their values.

The Role of the School System in Value Questions

To determine the importance of values in the school system, present teaching methods and the school cnvironment should be examined, first.

Generally school determines values rather than how students are taught. For example, when "democracy" is under discussion in a class, democracy must be evident in the actual management of the class and operation of the school.

The concept of "human rights" being taught in a class

room where there are no individual rights, reduces the credibility and the concept of "value question" to another educational fad.

The role of the teacher is at the centre of our concern for values in the curriculum. Should these be taught by him and if so whose value does he impose, his own ? or those from higher authority?

To a large extent, values are acquired through examples not by precept. Values are personal and cannot be imposed on a child unless he understands them. A child should be given enough choices and be allowed to make his own decision. Different teachers may ask different value questions, but they should be cautious not to insist on the "right" answer for any value question. A teacher should make his personal views clear to the student but he should not impose his values on the student. In any event, a good teacher will reflect values rather than impose them on a child.

Personal experience suggests that most students do not want to accumulate factual knowledge, but ready to work at something in which they are interested. It is quite obvious that the student's interest is aroused only when he/she perceives some thing of value in the subject or sees a practical application of the knowledge to be gained.

The school, then, is one of the most appropriate places where "value" concept can be fully expanded. A teacher must demonstrate those values in which he/she believes. In order to discuss the values related question in the class, it is imperative to have a better understanding of human growth. Class rooms and schools should provide proper environment for our children to develop some of the following qualities.

(i) Trust (ii) Honesty

(iii) Patience (iv) Flexibility

(v) Understanding (vi) Self respect

(vii) Respect for others

However the question that now arises is: Should the development of the above mentioned qualities be at the expense of the mastery of subject matter?

Some educators feel that the school can provide value lessons, only at the expense of factual knowledge. Others feel that "Value" questions should be incidental. It is quite difficult to polarize factual knowledge and human growth. It is not an either/or question, but both processes should work hand in hand. We, as educators, should not lay emphasis on one aspect at the cost of another. Our schools have a responsibility to the community to foster community values *i.e.*, to lead our children to understand and accept the values accepted by the society within which the school operates. Socially accepted value systems may be developed through self discovery. This implies the designing of a curriculum which caters to the needs of the community and overcomes the conventional gap between school knowledge and life situations. Thus, the philosophy of any school programme may be based on a new system of education that will enable high school students to develop skills, acquire knowledge which will enrich their life, and lead them to the discovery of knowledge. So, the primary aim of schooling is to serve the future i.e., to provide the students with knowledge which is related to their lives, and knowledge which they can use. Some factors which hinder exploration of "values" in the school system are:

(i) Examination and evaluation systems which involve only mastery of content or some skills.

(ii) Administration problems which need a more democratic set up.

(iii) Improper teacher training (Pre-service and In-service).

(iv) Double standards held by educators : what we say and what we do.

(v) The value opportunities which are in conflict with economic values.

(vi) Lack of opportunities provided to students for analyzing a variety of experiences.

Curriculum : What is it?

The term curriculum is derived from a Latin term "Currie" which means race-course or the body of courses etc. Websters' Third New International Dictionary defines curriculum as follows :

(i) The whole body of courses offered by an educational institution or one of its branches;

(ii) Any particular body of courses set for various measures (such as engineering);

(iii) All planned school activities including courses of study for organized play, athletics, dramatics, clubs, etc.

(iv) (a) General education

(b) A work schedule.

The above definitions provide a traditional view of the concept of curriculum which implies that the curriculum means only the subjects taught or offered in a training course.

In a majority of the developing countries, curriculum is regarded as a list of topics to be taught; a collection of syllabi from the Department of Education or University of the state and text-books in a given school, college or university. But as the purpose of education broadened and educators became more aware of educational problems and processes, the very concept of curriculum has changed. Syllabus is not curriculum but it is a component of curriculum.

The following definitions of curriculum by various educators reflect the modern concept.

Edward A Krug refers to curriculum as

> "all means employed by the school to provide students with opportunities for desirable learning experiences."

Ronald C. Doll, Hovold Rugg, Jaweson and Hicks corroborate the above concept of curriculum.

K.G. Saiyidain defines curriculum as

> "primarily an aid in the process of adjusting an individual to the environment in which he functions from day to day and the wider environment in which he will have to organize his activities later."

Alberty and Alberty refer to curriculum

> "..as the sum total of student activities which the school sponsors for the purpose of achieving its objectives."

All the above definitions of curriculum suggest that it is a total process through which an individual learns. This incorporates the 'course content' as one of its major components. However, it may be pointed out that the course content is not the curriculum—it is merely a suggested curriculum.

Kimball Wiles aptly describes the meaning of curriculum lucidly in the following manner:

> "The word curriculum is an abstraction. It means different things to an individual, the parent, the teacher, the college professor and the lay community member. Much of the confusion is encountered when some people consider curriculum as only the formal syllabus of the school, some others visualise it as

happenings in the learning situations, and some others envisage it as what happens to learners and the taught. The formal curriculum consists of the units of credit that are offered, the courses that are made available to students, the syllabi for these courses, the bibliographies and material used, and the evaluation devices that are selected."

Anderson refers to curriculum

> "..as the whole of the interacting forces of the total environment provided for pupils by the school and the pupils' experiences in that environment."

This definition of curriculum refers to life itself, and offers a framework of general aims and values, gives suggestions for setting learning priorities and outlines some content sequences.

Carleton Washburne defines curriculum as follows:

> "...enough to include any material or activities that will affect the learning, development, attitudes, or behaviour of the individual."

This definition implies that curriculum does not depend entirely on the extrinsic constructs. But theory plays an important part in the categorization and classification process. However, this definition suggests that the curriculum must help the teacher in accounting for the following questions:

1. How to organize learning activities in order to produce desirable environment for optimum learning?
2. How to utilise instructional materials to achieve the desired objectives?
3. How to evaluate an individual's performance, so as to determine the outcome of instructional materials?

The above questions are subsumed in the definition of curriculum by Gwyn. J. Minor which is as follows :

> "The curriculum is the means for attaining the aims of philosophy of education. Being a means to the end, and not an end in itself, it usually follows and reflects educational trends and changes in philosophy."

E.M. Draper suggests another dimension to curriculum:

> "The curriculum is defined today as the total learning experience which pupils have, in and out of learning institutions, under the guidance of the faculty."

This definition widens the role of the trainer. It implies that the trainer must be aware of the many ways in which an individual learns, and the conditions, experiences and procedures that best promote learning and growth. This also implies that the teacher has training in the diagnostic and presumptive approach, experience in the individualization of instruction and a fair understanding of the continuous progress system of organization.

In other words, the teachers should be familiar with the techniques of teaching pupils to think, to create new combinations from original data; to create and develop fresh meanings and to examine various possibilities.

Summarising the above views concerning the definition of curriculum, one may infer that the concept of curriculum deals with the three Ws of society, *i.e.,* What, Why and When?

What—What is to be taught to a learner? It implies quantum of knowledge, based on societal needs, to be imparted in a specific time.

Why—Why is this knowledge to be given? This suggests a rationale for imparting the quantum of knowledge, its methodology and its evaluation.

When—When is this knowledge to be imparted? This suggests a sequence of the curriculum.

Thus, curriculum can be defined as all those experiences of the individual for which an institution is responsible. It is concerned with What should be experienced. It also deals with Why, When and How a particular learning should take place and the atmosphere in which this learning occurs. The curriculum deals with human relationships in the local environment; it refers to the values, norms and goals of the community, society and the nation.

Values in Curriculum Development

In curriculum development, the term "value" refers to the things which are of the highest worth in education. These values differ from one person to another. If one wishes to produce a list of values for the curriculum, he might include knowledge in various forms, application of knowledge in daily life, and qualities, such as development of confidence in a child.

If some body else is asked to produce the same list, it is unlikely that it will be the same. He may not give the same importance to the same values. He may believe that the main aim of schooling is to acquire knowledge of facts for future use. A third person may attach importance to values which may be entirely different. For him, education is not a preparation for life, it is continuation of pupil growth; this implies that curriculum is not only acquisition of knowledge but that it also lays emphasis on activity and experience.

So, one educator believes that the major function of schooling is acquisition of "practical" and "ethical values", another educator may visualize that the function of school is to impart knowledge, while the third educator places high value on allowing a child to make decisions in the planning and initation of his course of action.

The above points out the differences between educators but one also has to take into consideration major differences between one child and another and between one social class and the other. Thus, values differ from area to area, from social class to social class. In other words a curriculum's values in a predominantly rural area are not likely to be similar to those in an urban area.

Curriculum consists of several strands or sets of values. The first strand may include basic skills such as reading, writing and arithmetic. The second may be the course content. The third may be the ability to evaluate, generalize and locate problems (application of knowldge in daily life). The fourth is the development of the creative powers of a child, and the fifth is the development of ethical and cultural values.

The total system of values is exemplified in the Schematic Representation No. 1. In order to illustrate the proposed model *i.e.,* Values As A Basis For Curriculum Development, it is imperative to make the following assumptions:

(i) The purpose of curriculum development is pupil growth and development.

(ii) The above growth may result from deliberate planning or random outcome.

(iii) Pupil growth should include physical, mental and emotional development.

(iv) Piagets' concept of pupil growth points out that the *stages of growth* are the same for all pupils but the age at which each stage is reached varies widely depending on interaction between heredity and environment. This interaction leads to the concept of "values".

Values as a Basis for Curriculum Development Students

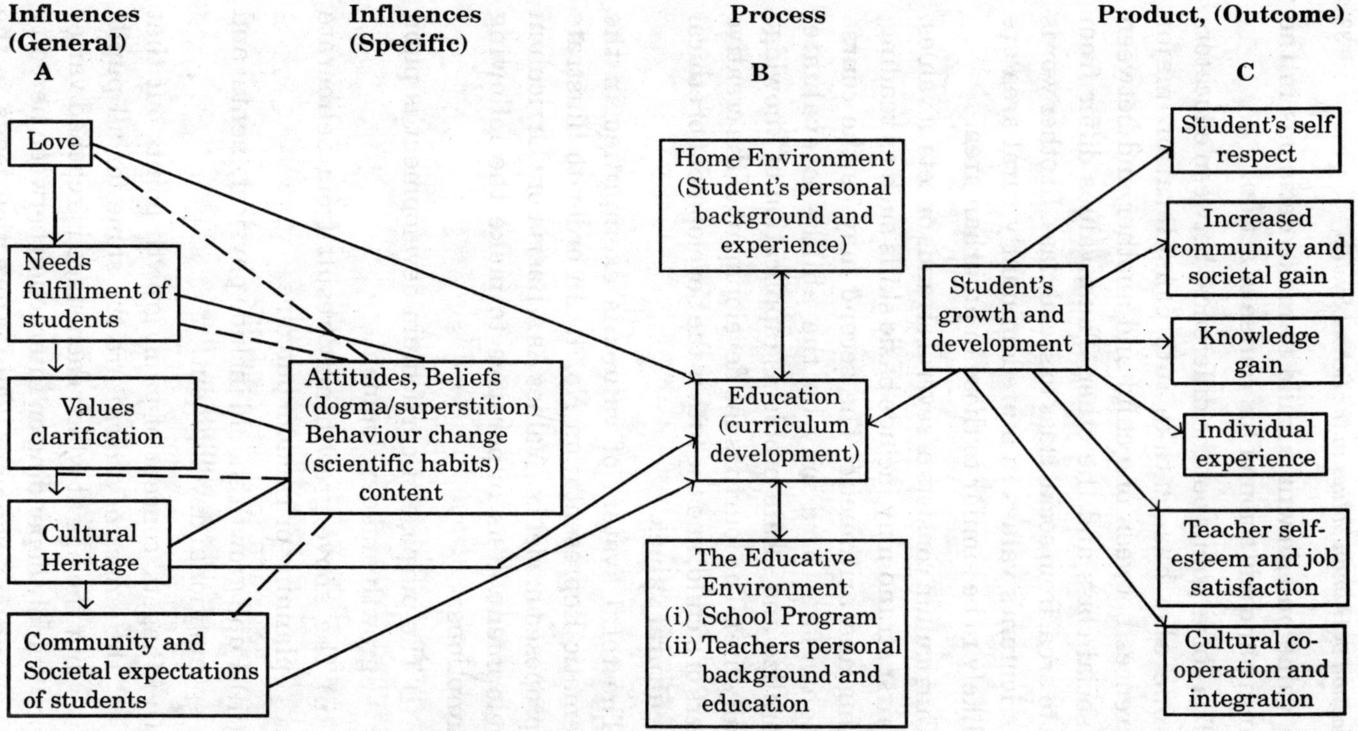

Schematic Representation No.1

(v) Pupil growth is an outcome of learning which may include the process of certain skills and knowledge.

(vi) Learning experience may fulfill human needs.

(vii) The teacher's role in the growth of pupils is to provide a conducive environment which may help them in becoming "functionally literate persons" and provide leadership to the community in order to improve their daily lives.

(viii) The teacher's role is to indentify skills and knowledge which are necessary for a functionally literate person.

(ix) Teachers can make some inventory for their pupils in order to identify the amount and the character of pupil growth and development.

Walter H. Worth's inventory of pupil growth in general may be helpful, if teachers want to examine pupil growth.

The Proposed Model

Relating to the basic assumptions of the proposed model that all learning experiences should fulfill human needs, the logical assumption is that the curriculum can be structured around the focus of love. To do this, one assumes that:

(i) Behaviour is acquired through experience, therefore the curriculum should provide for predetermined learnings.

(ii) Learning should be based on the fulfillment of student needs.

(iii) Learning should be based upon needs valued by the learner.

(iv) To develop value judgements, the structural organization should provide opportunities to make them behaviourally expedient.

Examining Pupil's Growth

Criteria	Questions
General Growth Objects *Personal Autonomy* (a) Selfhood (b) Individual freedom (c) Independent attitude	Does the child give any evidence of the personal autonomy as mentioned in the adjacent column?
Social Adjustment (a) Helping others (b) Sharing responsibility (c) Active participation in group discussion (d) Application of knowledge in daily life (e) Sharing with others (f) Group dynamics (g) Patience (h) Manipulation (i) Visual and auditory discrimination (j) Transformation of an abstraction into a concrete	Does the child give any evidence of the social adjustment as mentioned in the adjacent column?
Ethical Value (a) Personal value (b) Social conscience (c) Cultural values	Does the child provide any evidence of developing ethical values mentioned in the adjacent column?
Creativity (a) Innovation (b) Discovery approach (c) Developing leisure and recreational skills	Does the child provide any evidence of creativity in the behaviour mentioned in the adjacent column?
Intellectual Capacity (a) Maximum use of all his senses (b) Development of spirit of inquiry (c) Skills of communication (d) General and specific knowledge	Does the child give any evidence of developing the intellectual capacities mentioned in the adjacent column?

(v) The curriculum must be based on an adequate theory of learning.

Thus, in the curriculum the following qualities should be included that are basic elements of the perceptual field of learning.

(a) Self Experience

(b) Needs

(c) Values (cultural, social, personal and ethical)

(d) Attitudes

(e) Community and societal expectations of students

The development of curriculum must include aspects of cultural heritage so as to develop pride among pupils in their rich heritage. Students may develop an interest in learning to understand the world in which they live through an understanding of the subject matter. This can be achieved by correlating the subject matter with the cultural heritage of the students.

All these general and specific influences provide bases for a curriculum which should account for the total learning for the whole person.

The Teacher's Role

In order to implement the above model for curriculum development, programme development should be a responsibility of the teacher at all levels—state, district and classroom. Although teachers in most developing countries want and need all the help and advice they can get from various education agencies (for example in India-National Council of Educational Research and Training and the Departments of Education in the States) the ultimate responsibility should be theirs. The Schematic Representation No II. summarizes the role which the teacher should play in development and evaluation of the programme.

Teacher's Role in Evaluation Process

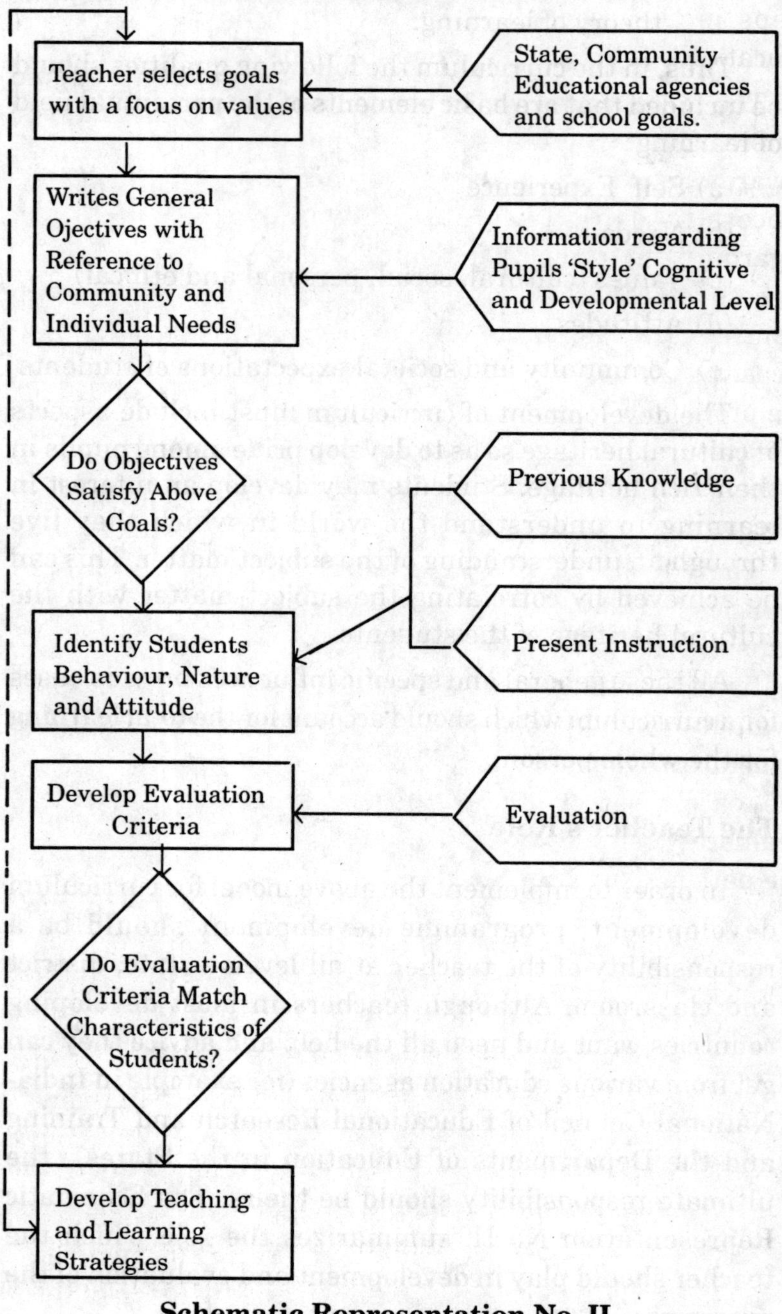

Schematic Representation No. II

In the schematic diagram, the operator in the series of steps is the teacher, with assistance coming from educational agencies, the community and other sources.

The process direction in Schematic II moves from the general goal structure, based on inputs from all levels, towards specific, short increment teaching strategies. The process takes into account all available information regarding the students, individually and collectively. The process can recycle at any point *i.e.*, information resulting from evaluation attempts can become an input into recasting the evaluative criteria. Most important of all in the process the teacher is the only agent close enough to the active level to maintain the closest tie between the development of specific teaching strategies required if the process is to work optimally.

There is no intent to minimize the role of external agencies; rather the intent is to make more effective the translation of all inputs, both external and internal, into realistic teaching strategies and evaluative devices. Evaluation methods should be determined by the goal structure and should reflect and at the same time influence the teaching process. In the absence of this relationship, evaluation becomes the goal, *de facto,* and teaching follows the path of least resistance.

II

Assessing Values

Strategies and Methods

Values are acquired by examples and are transmitted by what we do, not by what we say we should do. If we are to develop a process for assessing values, we must understand the background and environment of our students. We need to provide them opportunities to test their values. Errors in judgement may be discussed, but the teacher must be prepared to accept the values the students derive from the situation. However, teachers should be taught how to use various strategies for assessing values.

The following methods (or strategies) may be helpful in the evaluation of values.

A. Problem Solving

The problem solving method includes assessment of values. The following steps comprise this process.

(a) Selection of a definite problem

(b) Discussion of possible solutions to the problem

(c) Collection of pertinent data on each possible solution

(d) Careful examination of each possible solution

(e) An open-minded and unbiased discussion

(f) Selection of the best possible solution after establishing the criteria to be used for making a decision.

The above criteria involve "values questions" and also include mastery of factual knowledge.

The following criteria may be used in order to implement the above process.

(i) Choosing a Problem

(a) freely

(b) from a variety of experiences

(c) consideration of the outcome of each experience

(ii) Prizing

(a) satisfied with the choice

(b) willing to discuss the problem freely

(iii) Action

(a) doing something with the choice

(b) acting in some pattern in life

B. Scientific Method in Value Questions

To apply the scientific method in determining values, the students should demonstrate the development of scientific habits and attitudes. The development of scientific habits in the students can be identified by the following characteristics.

(a) Reliance on facts

(b) The power of observation, interpretation and inference

(c) The ability to locate and define problems

The development of scientific attitude could be demostrated as the ability to do the following—

1. To observe and discuss facts objectively
2. To be open minded and not to be superstitious
3. To review and revise one's opinion if the evidence demands
4. To think inductively

Success in developing scientific attitudes and habits depends mainly upon the teacher, and it is important that he always keeps in mind that students develop attitudes from examples rather than from abstract percepts: Students have certain values; beliefs in superstitions, diet, astrology, self doctoring and others like that should be dealt with when pupils reveal them.

It should be stressed to students that the scientific method is applicable in other school subjects and in the enhancement of their community and home life.

An important aim of teaching in high schools is to make the students active and alert citizens whose contributions improve the community life. To achieve this aim, the curriculum should have practical applications to daily life. The teaching of chemistry can be related to the problems of pollution, drugs, purification of water and certain other problems relating to the daily lives of the students.

The relationship of scientific instruction to the school's attempt to help every individual in this regard is admirably stated by Brunson and Dowling.

> A responsibility of the school is to help every individual to lead a worthwhile life. Those situations which can be better met by an understanding of the basic concept of science become forts of science instruction. Physical and mental health which are affected by sleep, rest, fatigue, diet, exercise, posture, and drugs can be assumed for the pupil. Self assurance, which comes from a sense of achievement and understanding of normal variability, is necessary to the best adjustment and can be built by the study of chemistry. Through an understanding of organic and inorganic changes, the pupil aims appreciations which help him to see himself in his proper place with relation to the world about him. By constant practise in recognizing problems, seeking evidence to be weighed and arriving at the conclusions, the scientific method becomes a basis for action with the pupil. Science can help present certain

fundamental principles which should be understood through partaking in and preparing for himself.[1]

It should be the goal of a curriculum to implement the above ideas.

To accomplish this, science must be taught on three levels,

- the facts level
- the concept level and
- the values level.

For example, in teaching a unit on water in science, the teacher might pose the following questions:

Level I (facts)

1. In how many physical states does water exist?
2. What are the common sources of water?
3. What are the methods of making water potable?
4. What are common solvents?
5. What is the chemical composition of water?

Level II (concepts)

1. Demonstrate via certain lab experiments the various methods employed in purifying water.
2. How do you know water is pure?
3. What are the effects of drinking impure water?
4. Demonstrate via lab experiments the chemical composition of water.

Level III (values)

1. Why is water important to you?
2. What would you do without water?

---

1. Brunson and Dowling, *Suggestions For The Teaching of Science in Twelve Year Program*. (South Carolina : Dept of Education publication, 1964, p. 47)

3. Is the drinking water in your community fit for consumption?
4. If not, make a list of things you could do in your village to improve the quality of drinking water.
5. What action, if any, are you going to take along these lines?

Notice the emphasis on the "you" in each of the above values questions (level III). Although questions in level I and II may recognize application in today's world, they do not become level III questions until they are directly related to the students' daily lives, environments and attitudes.

C. Working Towards Values
Some Practical Strategies for Students

Sometimes in everyones life they ask the question "What am I doing here?" No one knows the answer; people just make guesses. Different religions give different answers but a person must decide for himself. Unless a person's life has meaning for him, he won't have peace of mind. For life to have meaning, a person must have a set of values. By assigning values to behaviours and having goals, a person can find a direction for his life.

Making value judgements is not an easy thing to do, especially for young adults. The blame is sometimes put on the schools for not teaching the students enough about life and enabling them to make appropriate judgements. The following exercises are oriented towards these purposes. These strategies do not teach values, but give the student guidelines as to how to go about making value judgements.

These exercises are designed to teach the student

- what to consider when making a choice

- to feel confident with a choice
- to know how and when to act upon a choice.

My Favourite Activities (Strategy No. 1)

This strategy aids the person in examining his favourite activities. By thinking about what he likes to do, he will get a better idea of what he wants from life. Once you decide upon a goal, half the battle is won.

Write down fifteen things you like to do. They don't have to be important things, just anything you really enjoy doing. After you have your list, think about what is involved in each activity. If it costs more than three rupees or pounds or a dollar, put an appropriate sign beside it. Put the letter B beside the items you like to do by yourself. Put the letter F beside those activities you would rather do with your friends and B.F. besides those you like to do either by yourself or with friends. If the activity needs planning or organization, put P.L. beside it. Now rate your choices in the order you like them best. Examine your list. How do you think it might change in the future? Compare your list to someone else, try to explain the reasons for the activities in your list.

Discouraging Apathy (Strategy No. 2)

This exercise will help you to develop a stronger and clearer point of view.

Write down an important issue like corruption, secularism, cloning, poverty, drugs and describe your view in a few words. Now ask yourself these questions.

1. Are you confident of your position?
2. Have you told anyone about how you stand on this issue?

3. Did you consider several alternatives while making your decisions?
4. Did you think carefully about the pros and cons of issues and what consequences might arise?
5. Did you take your stand out of free choices?
6. Have you done anything about how you feel?
7. Do you feel the same way about this issue every time it is mentioned?

Now discuss with another person how you actually did come to your position on this issue. Which questions did get the answer 'No'?

Try another issue and see if your view is formed in a more orderly fashion, Is your position stronger or weaker?

How do your Values Compare? (Strategy No. 3)

This strategy gives everyone a chance to see how everyone else values things. It also shows a person where he stands in relation to other people's positions.

Make up a list of questions you feel are important or use one provided. Have someone read the questions and then vote on your answer. If your answer is yes put up your hand. If it is no, don't raise your hand. People who are undecided can cross their arms and those who do not wish to vote may pass.

Some questions you might use :

1. Do you think teachers should give homework?
2. Do you think cheating is justified in some situations?
3. Do you think giving grades is a good way to assess one's efforts in class?
4. Do you think schools are exciting places for students?

5. Do you think schools curriculums are designed for the benefit of most students?
6. Do you think schools prepare you enough for life after graduation?

Rating Values (Strategy No. 4)

This exercise deals with making decisions of different degrees. It's harder to make a choice if you have three of four answers to choose from. Ranking these choices from best liked to least teaches the student to compare the advantages and disadvantages of an alternative before deciding. This activity also gives the person practice in publicly stating his views and defending them, if necessary.

Think carefully about each question and state aloud the three choices in the order you would rate them. You may pass if you wish. Listen to the other people's answers. Afterwards discuss your choices and explain how and why you made them.

Some questions to think about :

1. How do you learn more ?
   - through lectures
   - through your own study
   - through discussion groups
2. Which do you think is the least important today?
   - poverty
   - military
   - pollution
3. What is more important in a friendship?
   - sincere
   - honest
   - kind
4. Who do you think has it easiest?
   - an only child

- the youngest child
- the oldest child

5. Which do you think is worse?
   - to be very poor
   - to be very sickly
   - to be disfigured
6. What would you look for in a marriage partner?
   - intelligence
   - personality
   - sex appeal
7. If you worry about a mark on a test what do you think about?
   - yourself
   - your parents
   - pleasing the teacher
   - getting into college
8. What is more important to you?
   - to work hard for the future
   - to love others
   - to really know yourself

Where do you Stand ? (Strategy No. 5)

This strategy is oriented to the strength of your feelings on certain values. It involves weighing alternatives in complex situations and including the possible consequences.

Have a ladder of series of steps drawn in chalk on the floor. The teacher reads a situation and you stand on the step which best shows the strength of your feelings pro or con on that subject. As each student place himself on the ladder, you get a better idea of how you stand in relation to other people's views. Discuss with the person a few steps away why he is more or less concerned about the subject than yourself. Another way is to have five or six different students and rate each one according to the strength of his feelings.

A sample situation:

A religious man gives regular contributions to his temple/church. He adds to this, the money he saves by cheating on his income tax.

In-Between Issues (Strategy No. 6)

Answers are not always black or white. You might have feelings somewhere in the middle. This exercise gives you a chance to see where you are when you are undecided.

An issue is presented to the class. Written on the board are the two extremes of the issue. Think about where do you stand. When you are called upon, briefly state your views (not reasons) on the issue and where you would put yourself on the line. Listen to the other people and see where they are on the line. Later a discussion may follow where you give reasons for your position. Did you end up in the middle or near one of the extremes? Where did the others end up? Do you think you have average views on this subject or is it very important to you?

Some questions to think about :

1. How much freedom do you have ?

   I have no say - - - - - - - complete
   In my life 1 2 3 4 5 6 7 freedom

2. How much do you like your school ?

   Want to blow - - - - - - - - - - love school-
   up school 1 2 3 4 5 6 7 8 9 10 never want to leave

3. How do you feel about your relationship with your teachers ?

. . . .

1 2 3 4 5 6 7 8 9 10 11 12 13 14

Real Friend Moderate Very Strict punishes a lot

4. How do you feel about your school work ?

   Worry . . . . Couldn't

   constantly 1 2 3 4 5 6 7 8 9 10 11 12 care less

5. How helpful are you to your class fellows ?

   Would never . . . . Always offer

   do a favour 1 2 3 4 5 6 7 8 9 10 help

On the Spot Decisions (Strategy No. 7)

This exercise gives practice in making decisions in a short time. It is also a fast way for people to see what others are thinking and their reactions to the questions.

A question will be asked. Think about it carefully. Organize your thoughts in such a manner that you can state them briefly. Listen as other people are called upon.

Some sample questions :

1. What issues have you recently talked about in public?
2. What incident in the news lately has really upset you?
3. What issues in your community upset you?

Discussion may follow giving people a chance to state their views and reasons. Any student may pass if he wishes.

I am Proud of (Strategy No. 8)

This strategy will help to build self confidence in the student. It also gives the student an idea as to the degree of pride he/she has in the things he/she does.

You will be asked a question about your pride in relation to certain aspects of life. Do not compare your answers to other people's but do try to get new ideas from them. Answer the question with the phrase I am proud... or I am proud that ...Try to think of things that you really feel good about. Don't answer with something you think you should be proud of but really aren't.

Some questions to think about :

1. What is something you can do independently that you are proud of ?
2. What is something in relation to personal wealth that you are proud of ?
3. What are you proud of in your school ?
4. What are you proud of concerning gifts you have given?
5. What are you proud of that has to do with something you wrote?
6. What are you proud of that relates to your family ?
7. What new learning experience do you feel proud of?
8. When were you especially loving to someone and felt proud of it?
9. Did you do anything to contribute to your community about which you feel proud?
10. Have you done anything to live by your religion about which you feel proud?

In the Public Eye (Strategy No. 9)

This strategy gives a person the chance to state his views in the classroom. It also, inevitably, forces the person to go over what he has said and evaluate his answers.

Someone volunteers to be interviewed and either the teacher or another student is the interviewer. The volunteer is asked several questions about his beliefs, feelings on certain issues. The person may refuse to answer any question but those he chooses to answer must be answered truthfully. The person may end the interview at any time by thanking the audience for the interview. The volunteer, at the end of the interview, may ask the interviewer any of the questions he was asked. The number of questions to the interviewer should be limited so as not to remove the focus from the volunteer.

Some sample interviews :

1. If you had a choice of how old you could be, what age would you like to be?
2. Do you smoke ? Why?
3. Do you believe in God ?
4. How do you feel about giving grades in school ?
5. Are engagement rings important to you ?
6. What do you like best/least about your school ?
7. Is there someone in your life whom you admire very much? Why?
8. Is there anything you really believe in?
9. What two things do you want changed in your school?
10. What is one thing you would like changed about yourself?

Sharing Experiences (Strategy No. 10)

This exercise helps you to get to know each other by interviews. By being in small groups, you can relate on a more intimate basis than in a large classroom.

Form groups of four to five people with one person volunteering to be interviewed. This centre person will regulate the interview by calling upon one of the group members to ask a question. The interviewee may pass on any question he does not wish to answer. The centre person can also ask a member of the group his reason for asking his question. The interview is over when the group has run out of questions or when the interviewee says "Thank you for the interview."

Two things to remember while interviewing :

1. People do not always want to talk about their personal feelings; you should respect someone if he makes the decision to pass on a question.
2. Try not to have arguments or start debates. These interviews are to help people express their feelings and for others to react to these feelings in a mature way. If you disagree with someone, try to understand his/her position; don't try to tell him he is wrong.

If the groups are small enough, and time permits, you may want to interview other persons in your group. This exercise is more likely to succeed if everyone has a chance to express his/her feelings.

Learning to Listen (Strategy No. 11)

Trying to internalise values is made much easier when you are in an encouraging and warm atmosphere. To develop this kind of an atmosphere teachers and students must learn to respect each other's views. Everyone has a right to express his/her own opinion and until this fact is realized in the class room, pupils will be afraid to voice their position.

This activity will attempt to help you accept and try to understand different opinions. The purpose of this activity is to aid pupils in understanding each other's point of view as opposed to trying to change someone's mind.

Everyone completes these two sentences :

1. I like to be with people who...
2. I don't like to be with people who ...

After you finish this, get into groups of three to discuss your answers. Each person in the group is to have the complete attention of the other two for a period of five minutes. During this time, the centre person talks about what he wrote down.

Things to think about during the discussion :

1. Give the centre person your full attention for entire five minutes or until he completes his presentation. Questions may be asked if they relate to the subject. Don't get off the track!
2. Try to make the person feel comfortable. It is not easy to talk in front of other people. Acknowledging the speaker's statements with nods or smiles will make everyone feel more relaxed. If you disagree with the speaker's statements, try not to show it. Negative feelings defeat the purpose of the activity. There will be discussion time later.
3. Try to understand the other person's feelings. Ask a question to clarify reasons for a particular response. Make sure you are not trying to put yourself in the spotlight. Also try not to reveal negative feelings through your questions.

After everyone has had a turn, think about how well you listened and understood. Do you have a hard time not saying anything when someone is making a statement you disagree with? Did you feel afraid when you were giving your opinion? Discuss and react to each others positions for another five to ten minutes. Did you feel more or less confident than before? Could you listen as well, knowing that you could say something this time?

Examining Alternatives (Strategy No. 12)

How many times have you done something and found yourself regretting it afterwards? May be if you had been more clear about your feelings, you could have acted in a more beneficial way. This strategy will give you practice in considering alternatives before deciding what to do in a specific situation. The purpose here is to get you to act more often in accordance with your personal values.

First discuss the things you have done that you regretted later. Now given a situation in which something must be done, decide what alternative is best. Take into consideration all your feelings related to the situation. What would you want to do in this situation? Write down two answers; one you think you would probably do and the second what you should do. Break up into groups of three or four to discuss your answers and try to reach a conclusion.

A sample situation :

> You are walking behind someone who throws an empty cigarette package on to the sidewalk. You are about twenty-five feet behind him. What should you do ?

What are the Consequences ? (Strategy No. 13)

One part of making decisions is by examining the consequences of an action. This strategy helps strengthen the ability to search for consequences which eventually leads to making better choices.

This exercise can be a follow-up to Strategy No.12 or by itself. Use a situation from 12 and write the key words at the top of the page. Make a table with three headings. Alternative 1, 2, and 3. Under each heading, write down as many consequences as you can, You may work individually or in groups. If you can only think of one alternative for a situation, write down not doing it as your second alternative.

Choosing not to do something will also produce consequences. Discuss your responses with other people and try to come up with new alternatives. Compare your consequences with other people's. Do you find your answers limited? Try to get as many ideas as possible.

Discussion with Self (Strategy No. 14)

Have you ever been faced with a problem and argued it out with yourself? Have you ever heard a voice inside your head telling you to change your mind? This strategy will help you to sort things out in your head by having a conversation with yourself. It will also help you realize that with value decisions also comes confusion.

Think of a problem you've been hashing over in your head lately. Write down what you think is right. After you have finished your dialogues, someone may volunteer to act theirs out. The volunteer changes from one position to another, as he questions and answers himself until he finishes his script. The person may continue his dialogue as long as he can or until he reaches a decision. This may be done in front of the whole class or in groups of four or five. People may ask questions of either voice of the actor to help him clarify his feelings. Try not to psycho-analyze each other.

Slicing the Apple of Your Life (Strategy No. 15)

How do you spend your time and money? Do you spend it wisely? These things are important for us to know if we want to move from where we are to where we want to be in life. This strategy also makes you examine how you live your life.

Draw a circle on your paper and divide it into four quarters. Each quarter represents six hours of the day. Now try to estimate how much time you spend on each of these things.

(i) Sleeping
(ii) School

(iii) Working at a job
(iv) With your colleagues
(v) Homework
(vi) By yourself, doing something
(vii) Doing nothing
(viii) Helping in community services
(ix) With your family, including at meals
(x) On other things.

You won't get exact estimates but you should have them add up to 24 hours.

Some questions to think about;

1. Are you happy with the size of your slices?

2. Draw another apple that you think would be perfect for you. Is it very different to the first?

3. Is there anything feasible you can do to change the size of your slices?

Try this activity with different pies. School, one subject, the books they read are topics you might try. Look at other people's pies and compare them. Is your pie much different? How? Do not get into arguments but discuss your reasons for dividing up your pie the way you did. Everyone has a right to their own way of life, do not try to change their mind.

Make a Wish (Strategy No. 16)

The strategy is to make you think about what you value.

You have a magic box. Inside there can be anything you want tangible or intangible. If you had such a box in front of you right now, what would be in it? Take your time with your answer then write it down.

Is your answer related to money?

Is your answer related to virtue?

Do you think your answer will change next Year/Month/ Week/Tomorrow?

What would you want for a friend?

What would you want for a favourite relative?

What would you want for the Prime Minister?

What would you want for the world?

Keep your answers and look at them again next week. See if your values have changed.

What Am I? (Strategy No. 17)

This strategy will help you to know yourself better. It will give you a chance to think about your life objectively.

Write a short story in your book once every two or three days.

Use these topics :

(i) What am I?

(ii) What do I want to be ?

(iii) I feel proud…

(iv) My most valuable experience.

(v) A turning point

(vi) If I was president of the world.

(vii) My best friend.

(viii) My children.

You may discuss your stories or read them aloud. Show them to your parents and see what happens. Save them and look at them again in a few months. How have you changed?

Chapters of My Life (Strategy No. 18)

This activity will help you to see your life as a whole. It gives you a chance to think of goals, past and present, and not living the days as they come. It will help you to be more aware of the pattern of your life and how you might change it to suit you better.

During the year you will develop chapters or pages for your life story by remembering events in the past. Try to examine these experiences in order to find important life patterns. Decide which of these patterns were results of conscious choice, outside pressures or of inner impulses. From time to time discuss a page or two with someone. Learn about their experiences and how they feel about them.

Some examples :

1. Who have your favourite teachers been; not only school teachers but anyone who has taught you a valuable lesson.
2. Draw a line with one end representing birth and the other, your age now. Mark off on the line all the turning points in your life. Put your age underneath each mark, and describe the turning points. How did they happen? How did you feel before and after? Did anyone notice the change? How do you feel about it now?
3. Write little stories about some of the following learning experiences
   - Learning to ride a bike. Who helped? Whose bike was it?
   - Learning to dance.
   - Learning to play cards.
   - Learning to love your brothers and sisters.
   - Learning to drive.
   - Any other learning experience you have had.

Strength of Beliefs (Strategy No. 19)

This exercise helps you to assess how strongly you believe in something.

Complete the questions on your own by indicating how you feel about the statement. (Write : *C for complete agreement; N for not at all; PY for partially yes; PN for partially no*)

1. Teachers do not get respect from students.
2. Man's nature is basically good.
3. Giving grades is a good way to encourage learning.
4. There is some kind of life after death.
5. Police are too brutal.
6. Women should have equal rights.

Break into groups to discuss your answers. Would you change your answers after listening to other people's reasons? How confident do you feel about your answers? Would you rather have stronger or weaker feelings? About which question?

Values on the Outside (Strategy No. 20)

One of the school's main problems is making the link between the classroom and the outside world. This exercise attempts to make this link by putting the students on the outside. Learning to make value judgements through experience will be a lot more meaningful to a student than ordinary class discussions.

In pairs, pick an experience or project you want to be involved in. These projects will be with people you don't know so there will be some risk involved. You have one week to finish the assignment. At the end of this time, everyone will report on what he/she experienced and discussion will follow. Please inform your teacher of project before carrying it out.

Some sample projects:

1. Go to the local courthouse and observe the cases brought in. How are the people treated?
2. Put on some old clothes and sit in the

unemployment office. Strike up a conversation with someone sitting next to you. Observe your own reactions.

3. Sit in the waiting room of the maternity ward in the hospital. Strike up a conversation with someone else in the room.
4. Find a neighbour or friend who is being abused or neglected by his landlord. Offer to phone City Hall to help him get it fixed.
5. Make up a lesson plan on something you think is important. Contact a local junior high school and get permission to teach a class your lesson.
6. Answer an advertisement for a job offer for a common labourer. Fill up the application and go for the interview if you are called.

Picture of My Life (Strategy No. 21)

This strategy helps students to think about where their life is going. How important it is and how they may want to change it.

Draw the outline of an emblem or coat of arms. Divide it up into six sections. In each section you will draw a picture relating to a question. The art work is not important, what you draw is.

1. What do you think is the most important thing you have done in your life?
2. What do you think is the most important thing your family has done?
3. What is something that someone can do to make you happy?
4. What would you want to succeed in if you only had one year to live?
5. What was your greatest personal failure?
6. What one thing would you like people to say about you if you died today?

After you have finished your emblem, break into discussion groups and compare each other's pictures. Explain your reasons for your pictures and listen to other people's reasons. Do you think your emblem will change by next year? How would you want it to change? In what direction is your life moving? Are you being moulded by others or do you have control of the building of your character? Is your life making a difference?

Making Life and Death Decisions (Strategy No. 22)

This is an exercise in evaluating people, also trying to decide which values are more important. It also gives insight into how difficult it can be to listen to someone you disagree with.

Break up into groups of four or five. You are high officials of your country. There is about to be a world disaster. Everyone is rushing to bomb-shelters when you get a phone call. It seems there are ten people in a bomb-shelter that can accommodate only six people. They are leaving you to decide who must leave. You do not have much time because you have to get to your own bomb shelter. With the amount of information provided you must make your decision in one and a half hour.

1. Accountant; 35 years old
2. His pregnant wife
3. Famous writer; 45 years old
4. A housewife; 36 year old
5. Her child, girl; 11 years old
6. Priest; 59 years old
7. Policeman
8. Scientific researcher; chemistry, 41 years old
9. Olympic athlete; track

After exactly one and a half hour stop, examine your results. Forget the actual contents of the activity and concentrate on your reactions. Was your group able to reach a decision? How well did you listen to the others? Did you let yourself be talked into something? Were you stubborn? Did you think your answer was right? Are you satisfied with the group decision? Why or Why not?

Communication Lines (Strategy No. 23)

So many feelings in our world are lost or wasted because people can't communicate. They are so worried about what they are going to say next that they miss the other person's point. Building values comes from considering alternatives. Considering alternatives comes from listening to other people's point of view. Only by really listening and feeling can we understand completely their opinion. This is not an easy thing, listening with all your attention to someone you disagree with. It helps in the long run, though, when it comes to investigating fully each alternative before making a decision. Also, understanding people better can only make life less complicated.

Break into groups of four with one person being the monitor and the others the discussants. The monitor helps find an issue that the others have different opinions on. As each person makes his statement, the next person must repeat the point he made before giving his own view. The monitor's job is to make sure this procedure takes place. Each person must be satisfied his point is understood before someone else speaks. The monitors job may change to someone else during the discussion. The discussion ends when everyone has exhausted his/her topic. A brief discussion may follow with the whole class : How well did you listen? Did you feel the meaning in what the other person said? Were you satisfied as to how much attention you had. Did you feel they understood your point of view.

III

Process Used to Develop and Evaluate Curriculum Materials with a Focus on Values

For many years, there have been demands for a more effective curriculum in high schools. The curriculum in most high school subjects emphasizes theoretical knowledge and rote memory. It is dominated by an examination system that stifles innovation and independent thought.

The literature suggests that this curricular approach and emphasis is not as useful as it might be to the majority of the population today. The introduction of new curricula in various subjects in Western countries could not really touched the problems of developing countries.

It is unlikely that any single curriculum in a subject will meet the needs of all students. While these newer curricula may go a long way towards fulfilling the needs of some students, it appears that something further is needed to meet the needs of certain other students such as the rural population of developing countries.[1,2]

What is needed is the development of a model of the process used to develop curriculum materials in various school subjects which are responsive to the needs of the majority of our students.

Here a model of the process for curriculum development with a focus on community Values is proposed (*refer to Schematic Representation No. III*)

The main objective of the proposed programme is to provide a systematic and practical overview of the school programme which may be helpful to students' behaviour and in their future careers. Other objectives of this programme may include;

(i) development of social responsibility,

(ii) attitude and ability to apply what is learned to community situations.

This proposed programme may relate to some significant aspects of local environment.

To illustrate the above process, it is imperative to discuss various steps involved in the Schematic Representation No. III.

Step I

Method used in Determining "Values" of the Students

(a) Research Questions : In order to develop the proposed programme based on values, answers to the following questions may be sought.

1. To what extent does the present school programme relate to everyday needs of the students?
2. To what extent does the present curriculum caters to future needs of the students?

To accomplish this, an evaluation questionnaire may be administered. Response to the evaluation questionnaire may reveal the significant needs of any new programme which caters to the needs of the community and which is based on their cultural values.

(b) Personal interviews with members of the local community.

Step II

Goals or Objectives of the Programme

A philosophy of teaching consists of aims and objectives of education in general. For an educator to impart

Process for Developing a Community Centered Programme

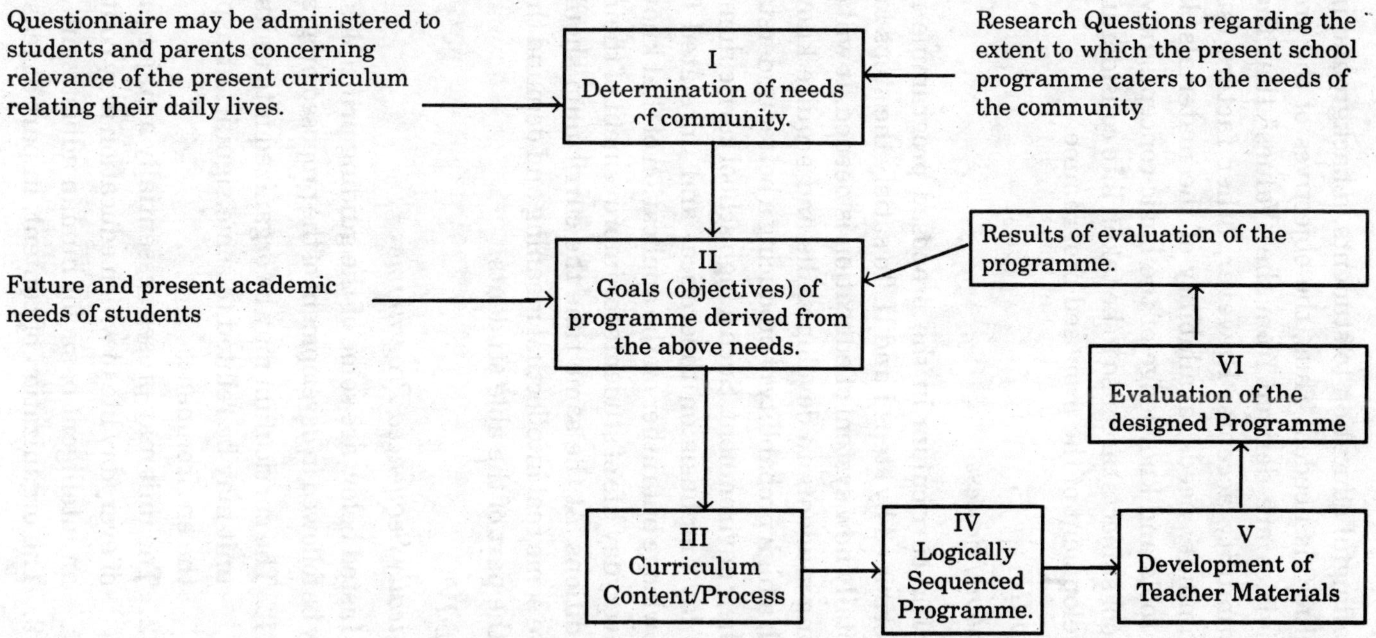

Schematic Representation No. III

meaningful education to students, a background in their "Values" is needed. Thus, the objectives of the proposed activities are derived from the "Values" that the local community accepts. However, other factors (such as community needs, availability of the materials, library, lab tools and knowledge of the basic concepts in various school subjects) are also to be taken into consideration for development of the proposed programme.

Step III

Content / Process

The curriculum in the proposed programme is thus determined by steps I and II. To satisfy the steps I and II, a totally new system of education is needed. It will enable young students to develop skills and acquire knowledge with a high probability of producing a better understanding of their environment. Such a high school curriculum would not lay emphasis on theoretical and unrelated factual knowledge but rather on the application of that knowledge to everyday life of students for improvement of their living conditions. At the same time the curriculum should also have some real intellectual meaning and demand thinking on the part of the able students.

Step IV

Logically Sequenced Programme

Listed below are some of the guiding principles which may be followed in development of the proposed programme.[3]

1. The curriculum may be organized into units. Each unit may be related to some significant aspects of the environment.
2. The unit may present essentially a major problem of everyday life to which education may contribute an intelligent basis for human adjustment.
3. The organization of content, in part at least, may

be in the form of problems or projects to ensure education in problem solving.

4. The distribution of time and emphasis to each unit may be determined by functional, social values of the units, its "teachability", and "learnability", the teachers' and pupils' interest in the unit, the local significance of the unit, and its value to other units of the course.
5. The organization of the course shall be such that it will lead to attainment of immediate and ultimate objectives.[4]

Step V

Teachers' materials may be developed and distributed to randomly selected teachers in the area.

Step VI and VII

An evaluation questionnaire for students and the teachers may be designed regarding the relative strengths and weaknesses of the proposed programme, its operation and existing facilities and recommendations for change. A random selection of teachers and students may be made in the schools for in-depth interviews. Additions or subtractions may be made in the proposed programme according to the responses made by the students and the teachers implementing the programme in part or whole.

Process Used for Developing a "Unit" of a Programme[5]

For the convenience of the teachers, the following model for the development of a unit of any programme is proposed.

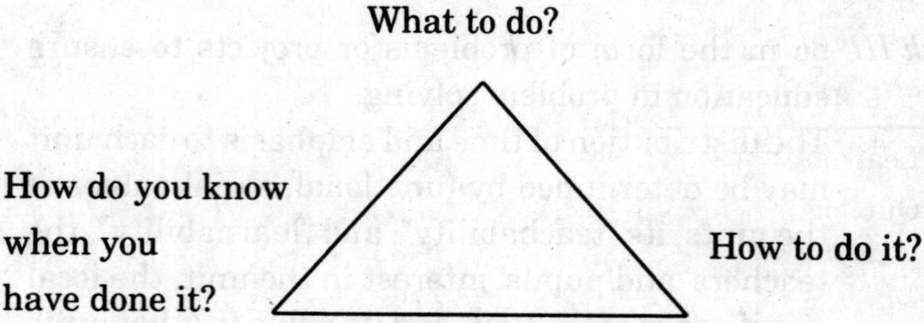

Unit Design Guide

In order to implement the above Schematic Representation, it is imperative to discuss the following questions :

1. What do we want or need to do within a unit ?
   —needs assessment
   — setting of specific objectives
2. How are you going to do it ?
   — student activities
   — teacher involvement
   — financial, material and human resources
3. How will you know when you have done it ?
   — evaluation

Task I—Needs

What area or topic are you going to focus on?

Write down students needs, community needs and school needs that relates to the area or topic chosen.

Task II—Objectives

Express the need in learning outcomes—the student will be able to demonstrate .....

Task III – Unit

Learning OutCome	Student Activities	Teacher Involvement	Resources — Financial — Human — Material

Task IV – Evaluation

What method would you use to determine whether students have achieved the intended outcome(s)?

Factors to be taken into Consideration for Validating a Programme or a Unit

Proposed Course

A. Description and Content

The following questions may be considered as a basis for validating any new or proposed course content.

- Does the content contribute to significant learning?
- Is the content appropriate in terms of maturity of pupils, objectives, resources and time available?
- Is the content unique or different from other content presently in the curriculum?
- Is the content organized in terms of learning theories?

B. Objectives

The following questions may be considered as a basis for validating the proposed course objectives.

- Are the proposed objectives in harmony with those of the curriculum?
- Are the objectives legitimate concerns of a public school system?
- Can the "needs" which the objectives are designed to meet and the problems which they are designed to overcome be substantiated in specific terms?

C. Methodology and Approach

The following questions may be considered as a basis for validating the proposed methodology.

- Are a variety of learning experiences provided?
- Are there provisions for dealing with individual learning needs?

D. General Evaluation

The following questions may be considered for validating the proposed system of evaluation.

- Does the system of evaluation reflect the objectives of the course?
- Is the system of evaluation in harmony with the school's general philosophy and objectives?
- Does the system of evaluation facilitate learning and teaching?
- Does the system of evaluation assist the student in self-evaluation?
- Does the system of evaluation produce information which is appropriate for reporting and recording?

Most of the above factors have been taken from the Department of Education, Victoria B.C. Canada Criteria list for locally developed courses.

References

1. R.M. Kalra, "The Chemistry Teacher in a Developing Country," *Journal of Canadian Chemical Education*, October, 1969, p. 3-6.
2. "Looking Ahead in Science Teaching Around the World." *The Science Teacher*, Vol. 34, January' 1967, p. 33.
3. National Society for the Study of Education : Thirty-first Year book, Part I, Bloomington (Illinois) : Public School Publishing Co., 1932, p. 209.
4. National Society for the Study of Education : Thirty-first Year book, Part I, Bloomington (Illinois : Public School Publishing Co., 1932, p. 209.
5. B.C. Teacher's Federation Professional Development Center, "Curriculum Design Guide", Mission School District Convention March 19, 1975

Research in Education Based on Values for Developing Countries

Value Research

What can today's research in education contribute to developing countries? To what extent are the results of present research in education useful to today's teachers in their classrooms? Answers to these questions depend in part on the nature of the research being conducted in education in developing countries. Recent educational research in most developing countries has not contributed enough toward making useful changes in the schools to meet the needs of their countries. Not enough teachers themselves are involved in the process of research and without personal involvement in research conducted in the classrooms, change cannot be initiated in developing nations. And it is a fact that the teachers of developing countries do not believe that they have the authority to conduct this personal type of research that can lead to useful changes in what is taught.

In most developing countries, teachers usually must follow the required syllabus prescribed by the Department of Education; giving the teachers limited opportunity to experiment and to try innovative ideas. The system of almost totally centralized decision making may prevent teachers from providing the most useful educational opportunities for children. Teachers must be free and must be made more individually responsible for providing the scope and quality of educational service that the people of each developing nation's community value.

To impart meaningful education to our children and youth; to help them better meet a variety of needs caused by the changing societies, teachers themselves must be responsible for more of the educational research, the results of which can drastically affect their classroom teaching. But as of now, diverse well intended groups comprised of universities scholars and other professional people have assumed most of the responsibility for development of research in education. And while it is gratifying to see these groups have wide spread interests and concerns for educational research; the system as it now operates leaves little opportunity for individual teachers to become involved in and to profit from "Value Research". "Value Research" must become the responsibility of each and every school teacher !

Teacher's in developing nations must be encouraged to make many of their own decision, based on the findings of their "Value Research", about methods of instruction and about contents to be taught. Decision making based on data collected through "Value Research" is the responsibility of all teachers who wish to act as professionals. The educational system in developing countries must be revised to encourage teachers to fulfill their role as professional educators. Also, they should be encouraged to plan and organize, work with colleagues, and devise new methods of instruction.

If teachers are to profit from their own research activities they must become familiar with the techniques used in Value Research. They must recognize the significance of their research.

Definition of Value Research

The activities of a teacher involved in defining and finding "Values" of his students is called "Value Research" in education. Value Research in education can also be considered as the testing by teachers of ideas, processes or materials in their class rooms. Here, action research concerned with individual and community values is called "Value Research".

Value Research is an organized evaluation conducted by various individual teachers confronting problems in their own work. These individuals adopt their own methods and practices and attempt to find solutions to their unresolved professional problems with the objective of improving their performance on the job. Value Research is the most potent means of improving educational practices because it permits greater flexibility in planning than is possible in an overtly controlled research experiment.

Difference between Value Research and Traditional Research

The major difference between more traditional research and value research lies mainly in who does the research and the place where the research is conducted. In the field of education, teachers, principals, and curriculum workers are those who do value research. The ideal place for conducting or testing an educational value, idea, or process is at the place where teachers are in a position to test the validity and applicability of learning principles and theories and that is the classroom. Here the teachers get to know best their values and those of their pupils. Value research systematically examines and evaluates the work of individuals who are engaged in the process of helping children to learn.

Traditional research in education is usually the responsibility of specialists related to a University or to departments of instruction. This research is often conducted away from the schoolroom, perhaps in the researcher's office. Traditional research should be more closely related to what happens in the classroom if it is to meet with an increasing degree of success.

Implication of Value Research in Curriculum Change

A major concern of value research is to find practical solutions to the problems which the students face in their daily life environments. In many developing and underdeveloped countries the majority of the population live in villages. These villages have continual problems related to sanitation and maintenance of an adequate water supply. Also, there are huge problems related to personal health and hygiene. These problems imply the designing of a curriculum that must be closely related to the real problems of rural life, presented in a way to bridge the gap between school knowledge and life situations. A curriculum built around the practical problems of rural life will bring the school out of its isolation and connect it to the worthy aspects of community life. To be successful, the school curriculum must involve the utilization in school of the child's outside experiences. School experiences should be on and integrated with the knowledge, information, and interests children bring with them to school.

Teachers can work with students to determine the curriculum revolving around community values. Teachers, especially in rural areas, can do much to better rural life through useful classroom activity. Through trying to relate school experiences to daily problems, teachers will establish their own position and prestige in the community as well.

Criticism of Value Research

One often hears that teachers in developing countries are not competent to do value research for they lack knowledge of basic techniques. Moreover, they do not have the time, for their days are full of activities. Perhaps lack of funds would also impair their participation in any kind of research. There is some truth in these claims for teachers all over the world. But value research does not necessarily require any sophisticated knowledge or special funds. It does not require much time outside of the normal teaching schedule. Value research as earlier defined is the "finding of solutions to problems" by educators in their classes. Teachers in effect can be value research oriented on the job. In fact, some value research does occur continually as teachers consciously make decisions based on experiences. These decisions affect what and how the children learn day to day in the classroom. This is value research at its most elementary level. More emphasis needs to be placed on value research in teaching.

Getting Value Research Started

Following are some practical suggestions to the teachers in India for conducting value research in their own classrooms.

'Problem' Definition

The first step in conducting value research is to define a problem that a teacher is having in his classroom. Problems to be subject to value research need to come from practical situations. Suppose there are students who do not like science or mathematics. These students are very much interested in other subjects. Thus, the teacher thinks that there is something wrong, *i.e.,* each student does not like the subject or the environment. The problem here stated is...to conduct value research, the problem must be defined clearly. Only if the teacher is clear about the problem will he be successful in this research.

Dealing with the 'Problem'

Once the problem is stated clearly it becomes necessary to obtain the best evidence to prove that the new methods or materials or strategies developed actually result in the anticipated goals. For example, referring back to the example of the unmotivated students, some motivational strategies like frequent reinforcement techniques may help the students to take more interest in the class. Once some evidence is developed, it must be interpreted. The final step in the value research is to interpret the evidence collected to evaluate the modifications made and also to find out about the future applicability of learning derived from the research.

Improving Teaching through Value Research

To aid the teacher in getting started to improve teaching through values research the following problems for study are suggested. These sample problems have been adapted from the material "Issues Related to Philosophy Objectives" distributed by the U.S Office of Education Washington, D.C.

Problem I : What changes need to be made in the content of the courses you teach in order to better meet the needs of the community in which your students live?

To deal with this problem, the following questions, for example, might be considered.

(a) Are changes in the curriculum truly needed?

(b) If so, what types of changes are needed?

(c) To what extent should school instruction be organized and taught to meet the objectives of basic education, as applied education or as a means of solving community and personal problems (practical education)?

(d) What kind of educational experiences will prepare

students to deal most effectively personal and community problems?

(e) Can I (the teacher) utilize traditional subject content to some extent, applying it to the solution of community problems?

Problem II : What level of literacy is needed for intelligent, responsible citizenship in free India?

To deal with this problem the following questions might be considered.

(a) What factors govern the literacy of the people?

(b) What valid criteria or measures can be applied to determine the literacy of the people?

(c) What level of literacy presently exist in the community and the country?

(d) Are there minimum essentials of knowledge (like social studies, science, mathematics, civics, etc.), understanding, skills appreciations, that are considered necessary by a representative cross section of leaders, scientists, and educators, for intelligent responsible citizenship in Indian society today?

Problem III : What should be the role of textbooks in instruction? Is there a role for auxiliary materials of instruction?

To deal with this problem the following questions might be considered.

(a) What are the present practices in the use of textbooks in each academic subject?

(b) Do the content of various textbooks meet needs of students at each grade level?

(c) Do the textbooks being used contain information directly related to solving the problems of villagers?

Problem IV : Should supervised study or homework be used to compliment regular class instruction?

To deal with this problem the following questions might be considered.

(a) What are the relative merits of supervised study and of homework in each subject at each grade level?

(b) What specific types of homework are most effective in promoting understanding at each grade level?

Problem V : What considerations and criteria should be used in grouping pupils for instruction in each subject at each level?

To deal with this problem, the following questions might be considered.

(a) What are the advantages and disadvantages of the various methods of grouping pupils for instruction such as tracks, and ability grouping within the classes?

(b) Is instruction more effective when students are grouped homogeneously or when they are grouped heterogeneously?

(c) How far down into the elementary schools should homogeneous grouping of classes extend?

(d) What combination of test scores and other evaluative criteria can be used as a basis for grouping students for different subjects?

Conclusion

In value research no matter what problems are chosen for study the most important contribution of the teacher must be the ability to interpret data, to invent his own study units and make them come to life by adapting to opportunities as they arise in his classroom, and to adapt his lessons to fit the needs of the environment around him.

While the advancement of education must continue to depend on research specialists, it is value research which will make education more meaningful and practical to most of the population. Therefore, an all-out effort must be made in developing countries to encourage all teachers to experiment, to devise new ideas for their classroom and to test their ideas. This is value research in action.

V

Values as a Basis for Curriculum Construction

In order to design a value-based curriculum for youth development and training, it is imperative to discuss the following aspects :

Youth – An Introspection,
Past and Present Response of the Youth,
Religion and Modern Youth,
Superstitions and Modern Youth,
Science, Religion and Superstitions,
Science and Values.

Youth – An Introspection

What does it mean to be young?

Is it a matter of excellent physique, rosy cheeks or a matter of will, determination and creativeness, a fountain of emotions?

Samuel Ullman describes youth aptly:

"Youth means the predominance of courage over timidity, of adventure over the love of ease. This often exists in a man of sixty more than in a boy of twenty. Nobody grows old merely by a number of years. We grow old by deserting our ideals."

"Years may wrinkle the skin, but to give up enthusiasm wrinkles the soul. Worry, doubt, self-distrust, fear and despair—these bow the heart and turn the spirit back to dust."

"Whether sixty or sixteen, there is, in every human being's heart, the love of wonder, the sweet amazement at the stars and starlike things, the undaunted challenge of events, the unfailing childlike appetite for what next and the joy of the game of living."

"You are as young as your faith, as old as your doubt, as young as your self-confidence, as old as your fear, as young as your hope, as old as your despair."

Response of the Youth

Swami Vivekananda wrote masterpieces about religion, science and youth when he was very young.

Galileo was only 18 years old when he investigated the principle of the pendulum in the swinging lamp at Pisa.

Shakespeare wrote masterpieces at a fairly young age.

Alexander the Great conquered the world at the age of 33.

Leaders from developing countries, such as Jawaharlal Nehru, Mahatma Gandhi, Nelson Mandela, Raymond Mahalebo and Lewis Goldberg sacrificed their youth for the freedom of their people.

Taking into consideration the responses of the youth, in the past, all over the world, it is the present status of youth in developing countries which demands the most urgent attention.

The youth in developing countries are in the midst of an overwhelming 'value' crisis. Seeking more of what western technology and culture can produce, some of them push for the adoption of western ideas and practices. They are faced with a choice of either staying where they are, or adopting the western value system in toto and rejecting everything they have known. This confusion and conflict results in literally tearing apart the culture of the children. Does it have to be an either/or choice?

Isn't it possible for the youth to amalgamate the best ideas from their own culture and that of the West? How does one accomplish this task?

A promising approach for dealing with the emerging value crisis among the youth, and students especially, is the rejection of the idea of imposing the 'right' values upon them. Instead one can teach them a process and a set of criteria by which they can themselves evaluate the soundness of their values. This approach might give the youth a set of tools and skills for sorting out the alternatives which are available and the consequences which may result, if they continue to live with a focus on their values.

Furthermore, the rapid changes in society result in a constant reassessment of values. Science, once regarded as wholly beneficial, is now regarded with some suspicion in the modern world. These aspects therefore need to be pondered over.

Religion and Modern Youth

One of the impediments to the speedy modernization of Third World countries, to the removal of social backwardness and the liquidation of vast prejudices and social conflicts, is obscurantism. Religion, if rightly understood and practiced, need not become a negative factor in national rejuvenation. Without going into the polemics of science versus religion, which characterized the thinking in the West in the latter half of the nineteenth century, it can be asserted that one can adopt a scientific attitude to life and yet be genuinely religious.

Modern youth may find it difficult to deal with people, especially in rural areas in the Third World, who associate smallpox with the wrath of a goddess. In order to have a meaningful interaction with such people, it is imperative for the modern youth to understand the relationship between science and religion.

Religion is nothing but the continuation of the scientific search for truth, at the higher aesthetic, ethical and spiritual levels. Religion-based on 'reason' has much to offer to humanity. Swami Vivekananda has described the application of reason in the field of religion in the following paragraph:

> "Is religion to justify itself by the discoveries of reason through which every other science justifies itself? Are the same methods of investigation, which we apply to the science and knowledge outside to be applied to the science of religion? In my opinion, this must be so: and I am also of the opinion that the sooner it is done, the better. If a religion is destroyed by such investigations, it was then, all the time useless and unworthy superstition, and the sooner it goes, the better. I am thoroughly convinced that its destruction would be the best thing that could happen. All that is dross will be taken off, no doubt, but the essential parts of religion will emerge triumphant out of this investigation."

The following conviction concerning religion by C.A. Stoddart Kennedy suggests a complementary relationship between science and religion :

> "Religion exists not to answer all questions or to clear up all mysteries. If that were its purpose, it would never be accomplished, for life grows, not less, but more mysterious as the intellect enters more fully into the truth."

This urge to learn more, the urge to investigate, the eagerness to explore is the very essence of being young. So the youth in the developing countries must perceive the relationship between science and religion. Religion should make it possible for young people to begin thinking, and science should make the thinking process rational.

Superstitions and Modern Youth

We have discussed above the kinship between science and religion and its forms for modern youth. Let us now discuss the concept of superstition and its relation to science, with reference to modern youth in developing countries. To accomplish this, it may be desirable to define the term superstition.

Funk and Wagnell's New Standard Dictionary of the English Language defines superstition in the following manner :

(i) A belief founded in irrational feelings, especially of fear, and characterized by credulity;

(ii) Belief in a religious system regarded as unreasonable and without support, a false religion or any of its rites;

(iii) Any popular notion attributing intelligible influence of some kind of trivial things, such as belief in omens, charms and signs.

Superstitions are generally the beliefs which are inherently irrational. As such, they are of various styles. Some superstitions are particular to certain localities while others exist all over the world. Most superstitions are ultimately connected, directly or indirectly, with religious faiths and rites. It may be argued that religious rites and faiths are not superstitions in a strict sense, since they find an origin and supporting reason in the religion. Superstitions which are clearly not connected with religious faiths are the real superstitions.

But even in real superstitions, one finds some sense and even a pseudo-scriptural explanation. In general, any belief that contradicts the accepted scientific principle and finds no possible explanation on the basis of scientific knowledge, may be treated as superstition.

Science, Religion and Superstition

Religion and Science are complementary because both deal with the rational process. Science and superstition are diametrically opposed, as science is a rational process, whereas superstition is based on unreasonable support.

Science deals with truth, so does religion. Religion deals with the truth of the metaphysical world, just as chemistry and the other natural sciences deal with the truth of the physical world. The book one must read to learn science is the book of nature. The book from which to learn religion is that of one's own mind and heart.

Superstition may be considered a mode of thinking which leads to escapism, resulting in helpless acceptance of an omen or custom. Now the question that arises is how may one use science in order to demonstrate effectively the absurdity of superstition? It is only by constant suggestion and scientific demonstrative illustrations that one may be able to contradict an unfounded belief.

Science and Values

Science offers mankind power over the material universe. Through the application of science comes the ability to build massive machines capable of transforming the raw materials of the earth into refined products, as well as multiplying, a billion times over, the muscle power of animal and man. Technology thus furnishes mankind with the tools to dominate his physical environment. It is natural, therefore, that such tremendous power of science will have a dominating effect on culture.

The problem is that any single mode of thought,

unattended by other modes, becomes narrow, petrifying and therefore incomplete. It may implant the seeds of possible self-destruction. The idea of science must be kept in perspective, infusing modes of thought and should be seen in its proper relationship to them. Overspecialisation, which excludes a general theory of knowledge, merely emphasizes a limited view, not freeing the individual to learn and continuously regenerate himself, but ensuring his perpetual lopsidedness. Science, seen in its proper relationship, however, offers an indispensable link with one's thinking.

It is hoped that no expansion of the ideas of technology and science will lead people in the developing countries to think that their past had been a lie and that their value system must be replaced entirely by one from an alien culture.

If the idea of technology or science can be comprehended in this context, it means an extended dimension to modes of thought. Only then the Youth in developing countries can be free to accept the idea of scientific literacy and not fear domination by it. So a clear concept of values should also be discussed with the youth.

The word value should not be taken in the economic sense only by the youth. It may also be considered in terms of realisation of intrinsic, desirable ideals and goals.

Now, the question arises: What are the most desirable ideals and goals which a modern youth may aspire for?

One may say that truth, beauty and goodness are the supreme and universal values which a modern youth may crave for, as they are intrinsic in character and end in themselves.

VI

Implementing the Concept of Values as a Basis for Curriculum Development – Recommendations

In order to implement the proposed model, improvements in various aspects of education are needed. Curriculum is not just a collection of syllabi from the Department of Education. The concept of curriculum also includes professional environment, instruction, and evaluation which have been discussed earlier.

However, the following aspects of education need serious consideration.

1. Education of Teachers
2. 'Relevance' in the Curriculum
3. Professional Environment
4. Curriculum Decentralization.

1. Education of Teachers

It is evident that the nature of the model (Values as a Basis for Curriculum Development) will place more responsibility on the individual teacher. This has some important ramifications for both in-service and pre-service teacher education. These are as under :

(a) More careful evaluation of prospective teachers should be done, and this evaluation should be continued throughout their pre-professional and internship years. Tests should be given in order to evaluate the practical knowledge of every day life situations which is one of the major guidelines of the model.

(b) Teacher training institutes should provide specialized knowledge and specific skills concerning the scope and sequence of pupil growth and development.

(c) A teacher must be aware of the full range of human knowledge with in-depth knowledge of at least one discipline.

(d) A teacher must understand the implicit relationship among community, society and the public school system.

(e) Stress should be put on techniques of teaching pupils to think, to develop fresh meanings, to critically examine possibilities, and to create new combinations from original or available data.

2. 'Relevance' in the Curriculum

In order to discuss the 'relevance' of it this term may be defined.

Can it be that it is concerned with the human quest-man in search of himself?

This search for 'self' begins when the individual starts asking the following questions:

- Who am I?
- What am I doing here?
- What is my aim in life?
- How do I achieve my aim?
- What are my strengths and weaknesses?
- What is my role within this community?
- What is my role within our country?

For educators, relevance is the connection between man's quest and the schools efforts on his behalf. A successful search for answers will occur only when learners join more fully in the life of society at an earlier age.

We need a fundamental shift in viewpoint, from seeing the school as a place where an individuals behaviour is fitted to predetermined roles, to the view that we should help the learner to acquire the knowledge, certain skills, attitudes which may help him to influence his environments so as to achieve these purposes. The classroom of the future must become an entrance into the world, not an escape from it. Instead of education being a laboratory in which people learn how to work and play, work and play become a laboratory for education.

Most students have little idea of the kinds of work will be doing when they become adults.

Every one needs the opportunity to learn employability skills, responsibility, co-operation, taking instruction, being on time, remaining on the job etc. Community visits, field trips, business tours, visits with artisans, recreational study, nature study, outdoor activities and cultural excursions are all vital. Exchange visits between towns, urban and rural and province to province are quite helpful.

The affluent should exchange with the poor, children of parkland with those of pavement.

Teaching for leisure, an ever increasing need, is best done through activities rather than passivities. One must learn to be a discriminate and prudent participant and consumer.[1]

In the light of the preceding statements it might be worthwhile, if every educator could suggest how this approach to curriculum might be translated into practical realities for the students in his particular subject.

3. Professional Environment

In order to implement the curriculum based on values, it is quite imperative to attract students with superior backgrounds, and in the long run to improve the quality of teaching for the students benefit, teaching conditions should be improved.

To accomplish the above objective, the following suggestions may be helpful.

(a) Salary schedules should be sufficiently high to attract competent teachers. Extra increments should be given to the teachers who are willing to work in rural areas.

(b) Teachers to fulfill their role as professional educators should be given time to

- discuss the philosophy of the school.
- work with colleagues.
- work with community people.
- plan career development.
- think, plan and organize.

(c) Frequent professional meetings should be arranged to exchange modern developments in their particular subjects and in education.

(d) An effort should be made to provide adequate resource centre facilities in each elementary and secondary school.

(e) Teachers should be given an increasing degree of responsibility for planning and organizing their learning activities.

(f) Teachers should be given opportunities to develop the skills of self evaluation.

(g) The professional environment in each school should foster development of a positive self-concept for each teacher.

(h) The professional environment should encourage active involvement of teachers in decision making processes.

4. Curriculum Decentralization

In a survey of teaching conditions in most of the developing countries, the following crucial educational issues are observed :

- What is today's student in our educational system supposed to learn?
- What are they actually learning?
- What does the study of school subjects contribute to students' educational developments besides facts, concepts and generalizations?
- Any skills? Any values?

The answers to the above questions depend on the existing curriculum in emerging countries.

In the present educational system of most developing countries, curriculum is a government responsibility. A few diversified groups like the National Council of Educational Research and Training (N.C.E.R.T.) in India, Educational Development Centre (EDC) in Ghana, Comparative Education Study and Adaptation Centre (CESAC) in Nigeria, Seamec-Regional Centre for Education in Science and Mathematics (RECSAM) in Malaysia, most of them well organized and financed, have assumed a measure of responsibility for development of curriculum at the elementary and secondary level.

The basic research scientists, social scientists, scholars and university professors, each operating from a different point of view, can, through a joint effort, establish clear cut aims and objectives for an improved high school programme in developing countries The task of translation of strong, but general, guidelines into curriculum development is not one primarily for research scientists or university professors.

To overcome the problems inherent in crucial educational issues in most developing countries, it is quite imperative to develop a system of education that will help young students to develop skills and acquire knowledge which will produce a better way of life for them and which will make it possible to lead the students to the discovery skills so necessary if they are to use their knowledge.

In order to achieve the above aim, programme development should be partly a responsibility of the teachers. *(Please see chapter 1, The Teacher's Role)*

To promote the performance goals, the process of selecting content areas and developing evaluative criteria and teaching strategies consonant with the goals should involve the identification within each area of those skills, both intellectual and manipulative, that are associated with successful performance.

If the previous suggestion that is the teacher's responsibility to determine the students level of development is accepted, it follows that for each block of work (topic, chapter, unit, etc.) the appropriate skills, behaviours and even attitudes should be identified to become part of the students evaluation for that block of work.

If the people growth and development in decision making is to be encouraged, then this should result in teacher growth and development in decision making at the same time. Both are complementary to each other. So, the teachers should be involved in decision making processes in their educational systems. Those educators in some developing countries who believe that curriculum development is a government responsibility insist that schools do not need to repeat all steps of innovations, nor are they equipped to do so.

However, an opportunity should be provided to those teachers who wish to get involved in a curriculum decision making process. Thus, the above conviction may categorize the teachers in the following manner :

The process of learning how to make decisions and of learning how to live with the consequences of those decisions

The intellectual processes which are involved in decision making →

- Recalling →
- Observing →
- Comparing and Contrasting →
- Defining →
- Classifying →
- Interpreting →
- Generalizing →
- Inferring →
- Predicting →
- Hypothesizing →
- Analyzing →
- Synthesizing →
- Evaluating →

The Process of Decision making — The Results

- Problem clearly defined
- Alternatives stated with advantages and disadvantages of each

Those Involved
- Pupils
- Teachers
- Pupils and Teachers

Each brings a different quality and amount of expertise to the process

- A decision is reached- Hopefully collectively or by consensus.

The results of the decision

The Process of Education

Pupil Decision — Making - A Developmental Process

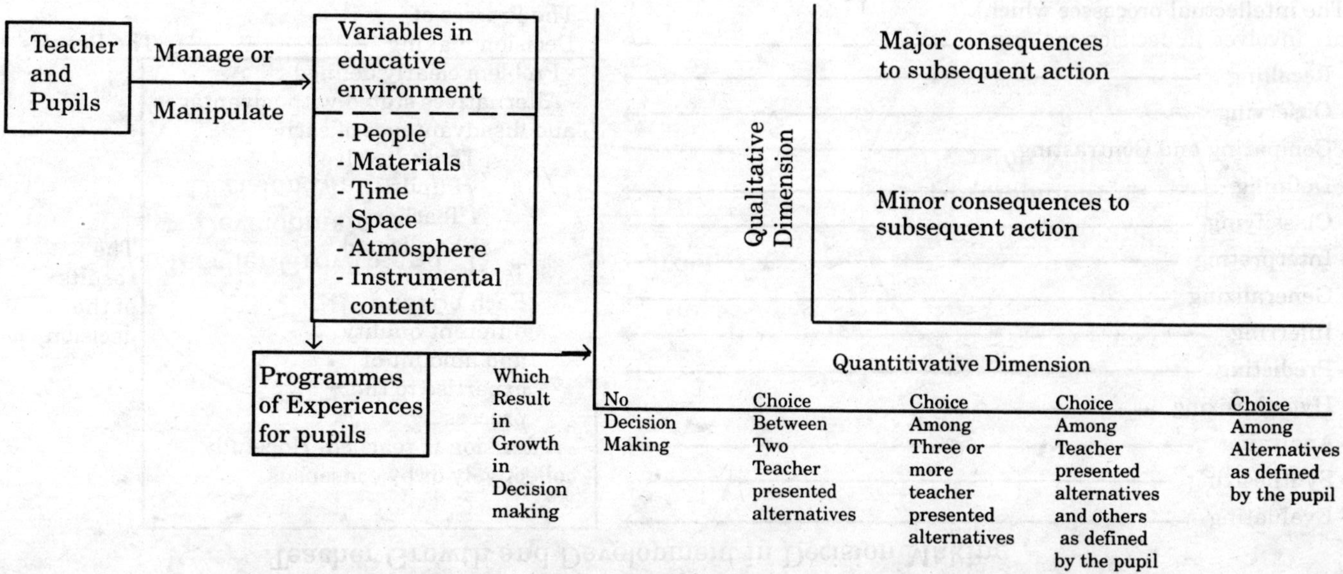

The above decision making process could be plotted on the above diagram as proceeding somewhat unevenly upward and to the right from the point of origin. Teachers can design the learning environment to satisfy the needs of the students so that the decision making process will be growth experience without any fear or threat

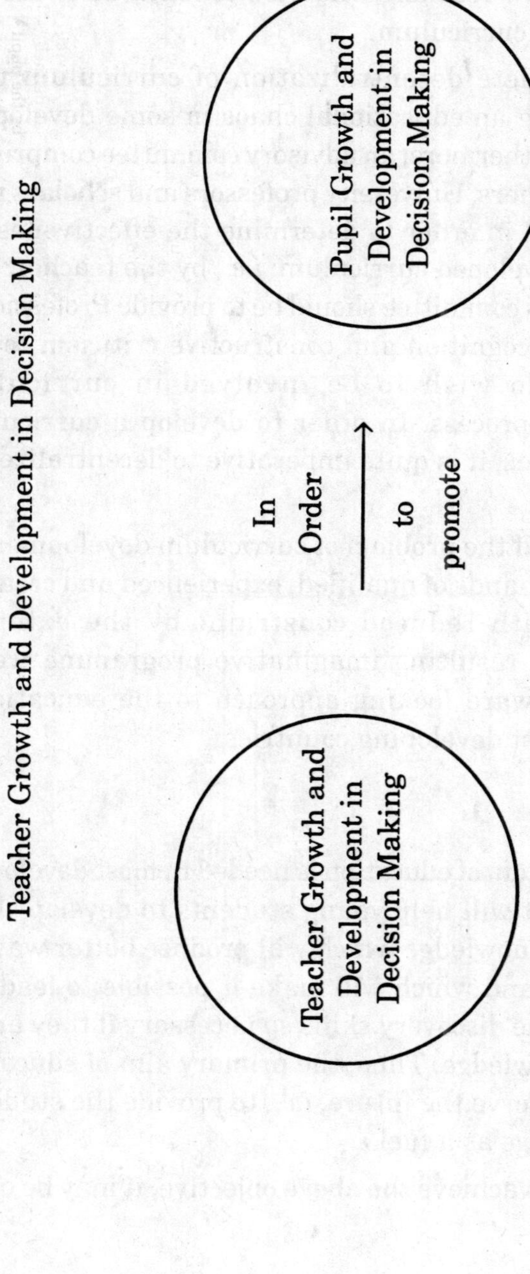
Teacher Growth and Development in Decision Making
Teacher Growth and Development in Decision Making
In Order to promote
Pupil Growth and Development in Decision Making

Category I : Teachers who wish to be involved in curriculum decision processes. (Decentralization of curriculum)

Category II : Teachers who wish to continue to use the Department's curriculum.

The complete decentralization of curriculum may probably bring an educational chaos in some developing countries. Furthermore, an advisory committee comprising of retired teachers, University professors and scholars may be constituted in order to determine the effectiveness of the locally developed curriculum; *i.e.*, by the teacher. The purpose of this committee should be to provide Professional assistance, recognition and constructive criticism to the teachers who wish to be involved in curriculum development process. In order to develop a curriculum based on values, it is quite imperative to decentralize the curriculum.

To sum of if the problem of curriculum development is placed in the hands of qualified, experienced and creative personnel with reduced constraint by the external agencies, the resulting imaginative programme would provide a forward looking approach to the educational system in most developing countries.

Conclusion

A new system of education is needed in most developing countries that will help young students to develop skills and acquire knowledge which will produce better ways of life for them and which will make it possible to lead the students to the discovery skills so necessary if they are to use their knowledge. Thus, the primary aim of education should be to serve the future, *i.e.*, to provide the students with knowledge as a fuel.

In order to achieve the above objective, it may be quite

helpful to implement the curriculum based on values.

However, no matter what is put in print to insure that a given curriculum will be executed in such a way as to de-emphasize straight memorization and emphasize understanding in the context of real problems and values clarification, if the teacher does not sympathesize with this approach or understands it, the course will be no better or worse than the existing curriculum. The most important contribution of the teacher must always be his ability to make interpretation, innovations, invent his own study units and make them come to life by adapting to opportunities in his classroom and living environment. He must be inventive in demonstrating examples of an idea from the resources at hand in specific situations.

Reference

1. Some of the above views were expressed by Dr. W.H. Worth, Deputy Minister of Advanced Education, Alberta in the Twenty First Annual Conference, Ontario Association for Curriculum Development, Nov. 1972.

VII

Education in Human Values

Certain Practical Initiatives

Peaceful co-existence and harmonious living is the *sine-qua-non* of civilized societies. Each nation should have its cherished goal to make every citizen a good human being as well as a useful member of the society. India has always kept in forefront the motto of *Vasudhaiva Kutumbakam i.e.* the entire Earth is one family. We should continue reminding our people this cherished goal of our (Indian) society.

With the passage of time, socio-economic and cultural changes take place in every society. We have to ensure that changes are for the better. Whereas the advancements in science, information and communication technology (ICT) and fast modes of transport have brought quite near the people of various nations, the unchecked freedom without ensuring duties and responsibilities has unleased several undesirable forces, the onslaught of which is being experienced world-wide. The Indian society has also experienced a feel of onslaught of certain undesirable forces from within and outside. In order to check further drift, the nation has to ensure operationalisation of a well thought programme of education in human values through viable ad effective modes.

Although in pursuance of the recommendations of the Education Commissions/ Committees pertaining to education in human values, the Education Departments at the Centre and in the States have taken several steps

---

* The author is deeply indebted to Dr. J.D. Sharma for his valuable contribution in this chapter.

towards value-oriented education particularly by weaving value-laden material in instructional materials, yet a lot more is required to be done on priority basis. The need for development of a well thought framework for education in Human Values has been felt for quite some time. Such a framework need to be operationalised with great ingenuity.

The Indian Council of Philosophical Research (ICPR) as a organized a National Seminar on Value-Oriented Education in 2002. Some salient features of its recommendations are as follows.

- Develop a Framework for value oriented education and define clientele to be covered.
- Elaborate strategies and modalities for programme implementation or programme delivery.
- The Government of India may set up a Task Force for suggesting a Framework for planning, implementation and monitoring of the programme of Value-Oriented Education.
- Develop relevant and need based material for different clientele groups.
- Monitor the programme implementation.
- Take steps for training of personnel.
- Besides educational organizations/institutions, cooperation of NGOs and volunteers may also be sought for operationalisation of the programme of value oriented education on a grand scale.

As an input to the plan for development of a Framework for Education in Human Values, studies on perception of teachers, parents and students about Education in Human Values were undertaken. The exploratory study voyage was conducted in some schools in Delhi, Haryana, Maharashtra, Madhya Pradesh and Punjab with the help of tools (Questionnaires) for teachers, parents and students, developed for obtaining feedback from grassroots level. Salient features of the Questionnaires are as follows:

Questionnaire for Teachers

This Questionnaire sought informational inputs on:

- Perception about a good school.
- Role of the teacher for inculcation of values among children.
- Is teaching a job or a profession?
- Values that need to be inculcated in students.
- Can values be taught?
- Role of parents for inculcation of values in students.

Questionnaire for Parents

This Questionnaire sought informational inputs on

- Perception about a Good School
- Significant features of the present school
- Expectations from the present school
- Role of teacher for inculcation of human values in students
- Time devoted (by parents) for their wards for (i) studies, (ii) other activities and (iii) inculcation of values
- Can values be taught?
- Rating on the list of 20 values
- Role of Parents for inculcation of values
- Expectations from the school about growth of the child (physical, spiritual and academic)
- Comments and suggestions for improvement of school.

Questionnaire for Students

This Questionnaire sought informational inputs on.

- Perception about a good school
- Perception about a good teacher
- Rating on a list of 23 values
- Modus operandi for inculcation of values
- Role of parents for inculcation of human values in their wards
- Knowledge about one's own life style
- Attitude towards societal concerns (*The questionnaire listed 12 significant societal concerns*)
- Perception about the phrase "Equality of All Religions" and "Taking Pride in Cultural Heritage".
- Role of Media, Music, Art and Drama to inculcate human values.
- Other comments and suggestions

The Questionnaires were administered in specially convened seminars in six schools. The participants included managers, principals, teachers, parents and students.

Synthesized Overview of Perception of Teachers, Parents and Students about Education in Human Values

First, a separate report based on analysis of feedback from each school was prepared. Later on a synthesised overview based on information contained in each report was prepared. Some highlights from the synthesised overview are as follows.

*Perception about a Good School**

- A good school has infrastructural facilities with sufficient staff.

---

* Analysis of feedback has provided a fairly long list of features of good school as perceived by teachers, parents and students. Here only some significant features have been highlighted for the sake of brevity.

- A good school is a temple of learning where entire staff (principal, teachers and others) are good role models for students.
- A good school strives for all round development of student (emotional, moral, physical); it makes the student a good individual as well as a useful member of the society.
- A good school provides good quality education through appropriate teaching-learning strategies and individualization of instruction. In such school, ample stress is given on curricular and co-curricular activities.
- In good school, every teacher acts as a good counsellor for students.
- One of the observations about a good school is that teachers and students miss the school on holidays.

Perception about a Good Teacher / Role of the Teacher

- The teacher should act in such manner that the entire atmosphere is surcharged with love, affection and mutual care.
- The teacher should evaluate the students continuously not only in academic aspects but also in behavioural aspects.
- The teacher should be creative and should strive for creativity in students.
- The teacher should use such teaching-learning strategies that may be conducive for sustaining interests of students in studies.
- The teacher should be a role model for students and make all out efforts for moral and spiritual development of students.

Some significant values and the societal concerns highlighted by respondents are as follows :

Personal and Social Values

- Honesty, Truthfulness
- Love, affection, friendly attitude
- Tolerance, Patience, Forgiveness
- Punctuality, Regularity
- Obedience
- Discipline, self-discipline
- Compassion, Kindness, Merciful, Sympathetic, Helping others
- Sincerity, Loyalty
- Dedication
- Dutifulness, Work is Worship, Valuing time
- Submissiveness
- Modesty
- Cooperation, Fellow feeling
- Good manners; Good behaviour; Responsible behaviour
- Benevolence
- Self-confidence, Self-dignity/self-esteem
- Morality, Faith in God
- Smart, active
- Simple living, high thinking
- Strong Will Power
- Creative thinking

Societal Concerns

- Basic equality of individuals
- Social or public good more important than private gains
- Religious tolerance; Mutual understanding
- Condemning casteism and communalism
- Equality of Sexes
- Stress on small family norm
- Social Service
- Inculcation of ethical and moral value

- Protection of environment
- Protection of public property
- Scientific temper
- Developing national pride in cultural heritage
- Dignity and worth of human persons; universal brotherhood
- Patriotism
- Respect for laws

Modus operandi for Inculcation of Values

- Generally the teachers are of the opinion that values are 'caught' by children by observing the behaviour of parents, teachers, elders, leaders and other personalities. However, several teachers are of the view that values may be 'taught' in the first instance through curriculum transaction and personalized attention towards students.
- The parents, in general, also agree that values are 'caught' at home, in neighbourhood, and in schools. However, the parents have forcefully pleaded that values need to be 'taught' in schools through a systematic programme of education in human values. Some books on human values need to be prepared for children and one or two periods per week for value education may be allocated in school time table.
- Teachers and parents should be role models for students. One of remarks given in a questionnaire (feedback) is that lady teachers should not be 'fashion models'; they should be 'role models' (in true sense).
- The parents, in general, have mentioned that they devote time towards studies and towards inculcation of moral and ethical values. However,

such time span varies from 15 minutes to 2-3 hours per day. A few parents have stated that they devote time towards their wards 'as and when required'.

- Some specific suggestions about teaching/inculcation of human values through curricular and co-curricular activities are as follows:
  - Preparing textual/reading material on education in human values and making them available to teachers and students. Appropriate print material need to be prepared for teachers also.
  - Teaching values through morning assembly, co-curricular activities in the classes and outside classes.
  - Telling stories, anecdotes etc.
  - Organizing plays, drama, debates.
  - Giving examples from books of proven worth.
  - By observing from time to time the behaviour of students and taking/suggesting corrective measures lovingly whenever and wherever needed.
  - By telling 'do's and 'dont's of good behaviour whenever and wherever needed. Value conflicts need to be resolved at the earliest occasion.

Role of Parents for inculcation of Values in Children

- The parents are required to play a crucial role in the context of inculcating desirable values in their wards. The parents are required to become good role models for their children. They should not show double standards in home ('doing' and 'preaching' differently).

- 'Mother' is the 'first teacher' of the child and she should discharge her duties meticulously both through words and through actions.
- Parents should devote at least 15-20 minutes daily to tell about moral values to their wards through stories, adventures, anecdotes etc.
- Parents should keep a watch on day-to-day activities of their wards. Corrective measures need to be taken whenever and wherever needed.
- Parents should not generally condemn their wards. Things may be got done through love and affection.
- Parents should keep in touch with school teachers/ principal in the context of progress and behaviour pattern of their wards. They should give feedback of their efforts to the teachers.

Equality of all Religions

- Generally the students believe in 'equality of all religions'.
- One should 'take pride in the cultural heritage of his/her country'.
- Knowledge of all religions and respect for them facilitate perfect growth of human beings. One should strive for universal brotherhood.

Role of Media, Music, Art and Drama in inculcation of Human Values

- Whereas some students are of the opinion that media plays positive role to inculcate good human values, others have condemned media in this regard. They are of the opinion that media plays derogatory role in so far as it relates to inculcation of human values.

- Some students have opined that media in neither good nor bad. It depends on how one selects Media Programmes.
- Whereas some students have shown preference for Indian Art, Dance and Drama, several others have shown preference for Western Art, Dance and Drama.

Certain General Comments

- Values need not be imposed; they should come from inner self.
- Inculcate such values that can be applied practically.
- Students should be capacitated to discriminate between good values and bad behaviours.
- Values need not be inculcated by scolding or by force. Good values may be inculcated through polite means.
- Educational programmes should comprise of courses of studies and programmes of education in human values.

The exploratory studies about Perception of Teachers, Parents and Students about inculcation of human values gave good idea of the pulse of society about the issue in question. Meticulously visualized programme of education in human values may be formulated and put in the system on priority basis. In order to check erosion of values in the society, the programme of education in human values needs to be operationalised as a crash programme with proper planning and continuous monitoring and evaluation.

Centre for Education in Human Values in Schools

- Keeping in view the importance of Education in

Human Values for the schools children, it is suggested that each school may set up a Centre for Education in Human Values (EHVC) with the following modest infrastructure facilities.

(i) A room may be earmarked for EHV Centre.

(ii) The Yoga Teacher or some other suitable teacher may be assigned the task of looking after the work of the EHV Centre.

(iii) Adequate resource material on Education in Human Values may be kept in the Centre.

(iv) The EHV Centre may prepare a framework for Education in Human Values in the school. The strategies for implementation of the framework may be decided in a forum in which selected teachers, parents and students may participate.

(v) The EHV Centre may organise periodic meetings of teachers to discuss matters related to implementation, monitoring and evaluation of the programme.

(vi) Short-duration orientation programmes may be organised for teachers from time to time.

(vii) A few periods (one or two periods) per week may be allocated in the Time Table for each class.

(viii) Some good booklets mentioning human values, good stories, anecdotes etc., may be provided to each students.

(ix) During morning assembly, teachers and students may be given time to speak on human values.

- Every year at least two programmes on education in human values may be organised in the school hall in which all teachers, parents and students may participate.
- The feedback about EHV programme may be analysed from time to time for modifying the implementation strategies as per need.
- The success stories of the programme may be documented and disseminated suitably. Precise reports about success stories may be submitted to the concerned Education Departments for dissemination on wider scale.

Our Resolve

- In the interest of unity, integrity and progress of the nation, education in human values should be on the top of the agenda.
- As regards inculcation of values in children, our motto should be "Catch Them Young". If well visualised conscious efforts for education in human values are not made now, our future generation will not forgive us.
- We should, therefore, resolve to start work in right earnest with the help of dedicated persons that are available in every nook and corner of the country.

Annexure 1

Teacher's Perception about the Role of School / Parents for inculcation of Values among Children

This questionnaire is intended to seek views and opinions of teachers about role of school / parents for inculcation of values among their wards. Both school and parents have to play important role for inculcation of values among children.

Please furnish relevant information in the following proforma. This information will be kept strictly confidential. If you, so desire, do not write your name on the proforma.

I. Identification Data

1. Name of the teacher ______________________

2. Kindly indicate your educational qualifications
   Please tick (✓)

B.A.	B.A.(Honours)
B.Sc.	B.Sc. (Honours)
B.Com.	B.Com. (Honours)
M.A.	M.A. (Honours)
M.Com.	M.Sc.

   2.1 Any other, specify

3. Have you obtained any professional degree? Please tick (✓)
   Yes
   No

   3.1 Please Indicate the degree by tick mark (✓)

N.T.T.	B.Ed.
B.A. Ed.	B.Sc.
M.Ed.	

   3.1 Any other, specify

   3.2 Please specify the subject (s) offered for practice teaching
   Subject 1 ....
   Subject 2 ....

4. Since how long have you been in the teaching profession ? Please tick (✓)
   - less than one year
   - One year less than 3 years
   - Three years to less than 5 years
   - Five years or more

5. Please indicate the subject (s) against the class (es) you are teaching:

Class	Subject 1	Subject 2	Subject 3	Subject 4	Subject 5	Subject 6
I						
II						
III						
IV						
V						
VI						
VII						
VIII						
IX						
X						
XI						
XII						

Questionnaire

1. What do you mean by a good school?

2. Please specify the following roles for teachers in order of priority (Rating Scale 1 to 11 i.e., Top priority - 1 and so on)

   * Getting involved in Activity ☐
   * Using a variety of resources and Task ☐
   * Mutual Respect ☐
   * Flexible Timing of Learning Experiences ☐
   * Creative Thinking ☐
   * Using Equipment that stimulates thanking ☐
   * Patience ☐
   * Respect for unusal ideas ☐
   * Re-evaluation as encouragement. ☐
   * Respect for differences in others ☐
   * Love and care ☐

3. Is teaching a job or a profession? Please state your views precisely.

4. Please mention ten values which may be inculcated in the pupils.

5. Can values be taught ?

If yes, how?

If no, why?

6. What do you expect from a parent for his/her ward in the context of inculcation of values? Please justify your answer.

Annexure 2

Parent's Perception about the Role of School / Parents for inculcation of Values among Children

This Questionnaire is intended to seek views and opinions of parents about the school and their role in inculcation of values among their wards. It is true that school has to play an important role for inculcation of values among children. The role of parents is very significant vis-s-vis that of school and teachers.

Please furnish relevant information in the following proforma. If you so desire, Please do not write your name on the proforma.

I. Identification Data

1.1 Name

1.2 Kindly indicate your educational qualifications

1.3 Please specify your professional statues

1.4 How long have you been associated with this school? (numbers of years)

Years

II. Questionnaire

1. What do you mean by a good school?

2. Are you satisfied with the functioning of this institution?
   Please tick (✓) Yes No

   If yes, please specify some significant features of functioning of the school

   If no, please give suggestions for improvement of the school

3. What do you expect from the school? (Please state briefly)
4. Please indicate your rating about the following roles of teachers in order of priority (Rating scale 1 to 10 i.e., Top priority - 1 and so on)
   - ★ Getting involved in Activities ☐
   - ★ Using a variety of Resources for tasks related curricular and co curricular activities ☐
   - ★ Mutual Respect ☐
   - ★ Creative Thinking ☐
   - ★ Using equipment that stimulates thinking ☐
   - ★ Patience ☐
   - ★ Respect for unusual ideas of the pupils ☐
   - ★ Evaluation as encouragement ☐
   - ★ Respect for differences of views and opinions ☐
   - ★ Love and Care ☐

5. Please mention the time devoted by you towards your ward. (Hours/minutes per day)

   (i) For Studies

   (ii) For other activities

   (iii) Inculcation of Values

6. Can values be taught Please tick (✓) Yes

   If yes, please elaborate your views in the regard No

   If No, please state the reasons thereof

7. Please mention your rating about the following values (in the boxes), which may be inculcated in the pupils. (Proritise the values on the scale from 1 to 20)

   Mention Priority

   - ★ Love
   - ★ Care
   - ★ Sharing with others
   - ★ Cooperation
   - ★ Helping others
   - ★ Forgiveness
   - ★ Obedience
   - ★ Cleanliness
   - ★ Orderliness

- ★ Good manners
- ★ Politeness
- ★ Respect for Elders
- ★ Love for animals and plants
- ★ Kindness
- ★ Honesty
- ★ courage
- ★ Fearlessness
- ★ Pride in ones own culture
- ★ Joy of learning

8. Please elaborate the role of parents for inculcation of values among pupils and suggest modus operandi for inculcation of values (Five lines)

9. What do you expect from the school about your ward's growth (physical, emotional, spiritual and academic)? Write one or two lines about each

10. Any suggestion for improvement of the school

Annexure 3

Perception of Students about Education in Human Values/Art of Living

A significant goal of education is to make the child a good individual as well as a useful member of the society. The task can be achieved substantially through well formulated educational programme and its implementation meticulously.

The apex educational organisations at the national level and at the State level have been endeavouring to make provision of relevant and need based school education for students. The educational programmes (both curricular and co-curricular) are designed to meet the goals of education. Among other things the study materials (textbooks, supplementary reading materials etc.) and teaching-learning strategies are supposed to be conducive to enrichment of lives of students. there are several do's and dont's (related to human values) for the students for becoming good citizens. They come to know about these do's and dont's during the period their education, mainly in the educational institutions.

The present **Questionnaire** is designed to know the perception of students about human values and education in human values/ art of living. The Questionnaire is in two Parts.

- Part I relates to identification information about the student.
- Part II relates to perception of students about human values and values education.

Questionnaire for Students

Part I

Identification Date

Name of Student ______________________

Father's Name ______________________

Date of Birth Date Month Year

Class in which studying ______________________

Name and Address of the school ______________________

Residential Address __________________________________

____

Part II

Perception of Students about Human Values and Value Education

1. What is your perception about a good school?
   Please Tick (✓) as per your perception.

A good school is one:	Yes	No
1.1 Where child gets good education	☐	☐
1.2 Which has facillities for imparting good education	☐	☐
1.3 Which inculcates moral, human and spiritual values in the child	☐	☐
1.4 Which prepares the students to face challenges in real life	☐	☐
1.5 Which enriches the student with information on rich culture and cultural heritage of the countary	☐	☐
1.6 Which gives full freedom to students without Responsibility/accountability	☐	☐
1.7 Which allows students to take part in decision making	☐	☐

* Any other comments/suggestions about good school (Mention below)

2. What is your perception about a good teacher?
   Please tick

A good teacher is one:	Yes	No
2.1 Who gives love and affection to students	☐	☐

2.3	Who pays attention towards each students as per need	☐	☐
2.4	Who listens patiently the ideas of students and gives responses calmly.	☐	☐
2.5	Who motivates and encourages the students for better achievement	☐	☐
2.6	Who has a good moral character	☐	☐
2.7	Who advises about desirable do's and dont's that may enrich the lives of students.	☐	☐
2.8	Who is very strict and regid.	☐	☐

* Any other comments/suggestion about a good teacher (Mention below)

3. What are the Values that need to be inculcated in students? Please tick those that are appropriate according to you. The Values that need to be inculcated may be :

		Yes	No
3.1	Universal brotherhood	☐	☐
3.2	Peace	☐	☐
3.3	Patriotism	☐	☐
3.4	Equality	☐	☐
3.5	Cooperation	☐	☐
3.6	Helping others	☐	☐
3.7	Compassion	☐	☐
3.8	Adjustment with others	☐	☐
3.9	Patience	☐	☐
3.10	Obedience	☐	☐
3.11	Punctuality	☐	☐
3.12	Dedication	☐	☐
3.13	Hard Work	☐	☐
3.14	Honesty	☐	☐
3.15	Courage	☐	☐
3.16	Dutiful	☐	☐
3.17	Forgiveness	☐	☐
3.18	Submissive	☐	☐

	Yes	No
3.19 Cleanliness	☐	☐
3.20 Protection of Envioronment	☐	☐
3.21 Scientific Temper	☐	☐
3.22 Loving nature	☐	☐
3.23 Respect for Elders	☐	☐

* Any other comments and suggestions about inculcation of values (Mention below)

4. How the values may be inculcated in the students? Please tick the methods that are appropriate according to you.

The Values may be inculcated in the following ways:

	Yes	No
4.1 Teacher should 'teach' values (i.e., this is good, this is not good; do it, don't do it; these are good behaviours, these are bad habits etc.)	☐	☐
4.2 Techer should himself be a good role model and his/her good values may be 'caught' by the students	☐	☐
4.3 Values may be 'taught' and 'caught' both.	☐	☐
4.4 Teacher should tell stories, poems, anecdotes etc., that contain or reflect good values to be followed of practised.	☐	☐
4.5 Teacher should organise co-curricular or extra-curricular activities within the school and/or outside the school that may be conducive for inculcation of good values.	☐	☐
4.6 Some good values may be taught or discussed in the morning assembly in school on each working day.	☐	☐

4.7 At least one period per week for Education in Human Values need to be allocated in the Time Table.	☐	☐	

* Any other comments/suggestions regarding inculcation of values in students?

5. Perception of students about Role of Parents for inculcation of human values

Please tick the appropriate.	Yes	No	Don't-Know
5.1 Do you feel that parents give you good advice for enrichment of your life with good values?	☐	☐	☐
5.2 Do you feel that parents need to be good role models for their children?	☐	☐	☐
5.3 Do you feel that there should be consistency in preaching and acts of parents (i.e., whatever they prech should themselves practise those)	☐	☐	☐
5.4 Do you feel that parents need not insist their children to inculcate/ follow certain ideals/values?	☐	☐	☐
5.5 Do you feel that the parents should give full freedom to their children to adopt or not to adopt valules generally prevailing in the society?	☐	☐	☐

6. **Knowing your Lifestyle**

Think carefully about the following statements and give them rank (1 or 2 or 3), in order you like/agree, against the statements given below.

Rank Criteria	**Rank**
Most Favourable	1
Just Favourable	2
Least Favourable	3

S.No.	**Statements**	**Rank**
1.	**I would like to be friendly with the following:**	
	1.1 Who have lot of money and can spend on me.	
	1.2 Who are very rich, though they have bad habits.	
	1.3 Who are not rich but have good moral character	
2.	**I would like to:**	
	2.1 Have an instant rise by fair or foul means.	
	2.2 Have more money, good clothes, and earn a position of prestige in the society even by dubious means.	
	2.3 Have money by hard work and honest means.	
3.	**I would prefer:**	
	3.1 Love and affection in the family even if pocket money given to me is less.	
	3.2 Lack of love and affection in the family but would like to have more Pocket money, more parties and drinks.	
	3.3 Modern life style discarding social values like truthfulness, honesty, sincerity and hard work.	

4. **What is important in friendship?**
   4.1 Sincerity
   4.2 Honesty
   4.3 Eat, drink and be marry
   (drinking wine, smoking, gambling etc.)

5. **What is more important to you in your life?**
   5.1 To work hard for making the future bright.
   5.2 To become rich instantly by any means.
   5.3 To really know about your inner self.

6. **What is more significant for you?**
   6.1 Total freedom with no restrictions or checks.
   6.2 Freedom with responsibility
   6.3 Working for welfare of the community.

7. **Attitude towards societal concerns**

There are certain societal concerns. It has been observed that individuals have/show different attitudes towards the societal concerns consciously or unconsciously or due to certain biases/prejudices.

Please tick against the following statements as per your thinking or perception. Please give free and frank opinion.

S.No.	Statement	Agree	Disagree	Undecided
1.	There is basic equality of individuals			
2.	Social good is more important that private gains			
3.	Equal (positive) respect needs to given to all religions.			
4.	Religious communalism, sectarian conflicts and prejudices need to be condemned in the interest of social harmony.			

5. Efforts need to be made enthusiastically for peaceful co-existence with all groups.
6. Students should be apprised properly about the rich Indian Cultural Heritage along with other informational inputs.
7. India's composite culture and unity in diversity needs to be appreciated.
8. Both men and women should enjoy full equality in all walks of life
9. Social and economic disparities need to be removed to the extent possible.
10. Stress needs to be given on small family norm.
11. Scocial evils like untouchability, dowry and child marriage need tobe condemned.
12. One should be prepared to sacrifice narrow loyalties and interests for maintaining and strengthening national unity and integrity.

8. **Perception of Students about significance of the phrases "Equality of All Religion: and "Taking Pride in Cultural Herigate"**

Please tick the appropriate.	**Yes**	**No**	**Undecided**
8.1 Do you agree that all religions are equal?			

8.1.1 What are the major religions of the World and mention title of one main book of each religion.

S.No.	Name of the Religion	Name of Book
1.		
2.		
3.		
4.		
5.		

8.2 Should one eulogies, (Praise/commend) one's own religion vis-à-vis other religions?

8.3 Should One take pride in the cultural heritage of his country?

8.4 Should significant past cultural events of one's own country be highlighted in the study materials of concerned subjects?

* Write your overall comments and suggestions about "equality of all religions" and "taking pride in cultural heritage."

9. **Perception of students about the Role of Media, Music, Art and Drama to inculcate human values.**

Please tick the appropriate.

9.1 **What is your overall perception about role of media (TV, Radio) for inculcation of human values?** Yes No Undecided

9.1.1 Media plays positive role for inculcation of good human values.

9.1.2 Media plays derogatory rold in so far as it relates to human values.

	Yes	No
9.2 **Do you like:**		
9.2.1 Indian Classical Music		
9.2.2 Present form of Indian Music		
9.2.3 Pop Music (Western)		
9.3 **Do you like:**		
9.3.1 Indian Art and Drama		
9.3.2 Western Art and Drama		
9.3.3 Modern Art		

* Overall comments/suggestions about role of Media, Music, Art and Drama to inculcate values.

10. Overall comments and Suggestions

    Write your overall comments and suggestions about Education in Human Values. Please be precise and brief comments/suggestions may be written in not more than 200 words.

VIII

Evaluation in Value Education

The school curricula is required to give adequate emphasis to scholastic and co-scholastic aspects. As regards the co-scholastic aspects, the school curricula is required to give adequate thrust to:

(i) Inculcation and sustenance of personal, social, national and spiritual values and values like cleanliness and punctuality, good conduct, tolerance and justice, a sense of national identity and respect for law and order and truthfulness.

(ii) Fundamental Duties and the co-curricular areas mentioned in the National Policy on Education (1986) at all stages of school education may be given due emphasis.

Although Value Education may not form a separate subject of study, these are to be judiciously integrated with all the subjects of study in the scholastic areas and all the activities and programme in the co-scholastic areas. It has to be ensured that the objectives of Value Education would be directly and indirectly achieved in class room and at the school assembly places etc.

Theoretical Interpretation of Concept of Evaluation in Value Education

Linda and Richard Eyre suggest inculcation of values among children means "Teaching your Children Sensitivity." Values are manifestation of determination of sensitivity towards other fellow human beings.

In evaluation terms, the sensitivity can be described as follows:

U +	O +	F +	C +	D =	S
Understanding	Observing	Feeling	Communication	Doing =	Sensitivity

The concept of evaluation in Value Education includes the above mentioned processes which suggests performance based evaluation, behavioural modification and attitudinal change in the students.

Evaluation of Students in Value Education

In the light of the theoretical interpretation of concept of Evaluation in Value Education, it is imperative to have a continuous process of evaluation which needs to be operationalised and monitored meticulously.

The following modus operandi for pupil evaluation in Value Education is suggested which is not prescriptive in nature:

Some schools have ear marked periods for Value Education / Moral Education. These programmes in schools include reading material for students with suitable teaching learning strategies. The pupil evaluation in value education may include both:

(i) written test;

(ii) performance based evaluation;

(iii) observations by teachers in an objective manner;

Such evaluation would enable the institution to assess theoretical understanding of values by students and their behaviour pattern.

In the school curriculum frame work, generally specific periods are not ear marked for value education. The assumptions about Value Education in school education programmes are as follows:

(i) As per curriculum frame work, selection and presentation of content in the school text books on different subjects interalia take care of education in human values. Human values and societal concerns are generally appropriately reflected in the school text books.

(ii) While transacting school curricular, the teachers and interalia are required to be taken care of inculcation of human values in students.

Evaluation Criteria Frame for Value Education

For pupil evaluation in the context of value education, simply written tests would not serve the purpose. The students behaviour in various situations will have to be observed carefully by the teachers over a period of time.

The teacher is required to keep meticulously the record of personal and social values of each student. He / She may note down the behaviour patterns of each student separately in a pre-designed proforma.

The students 'Record of Values' proforma may include:-

(i) a statement showing the values appropriately classified and

(ii) columns for recording brief observations (wherever needed) and grading based on observations in various situations.

An sample profoma for students Record of Values is given :

Students Record of Values

Name of the student ________________ Class _________

Academic Year __________

Rating: A / B / C / D

A - Outstanding B - Very Good

C - Good D - Needs improvement

S. No.	Values/Criteria	July-Sep.	Oct.-Dec.	Jan.-Mar.	Remarks
I	**Love**				
1.1	Equality				
1.2	Co-operation				
1.3	Kindness				
II	**Courage**				
2.1	Confidence				
2.2	Determination				
2.3	Fearlessness				
III	**Peaceful co-existence**				
3.1	Patience/Tolerance				
3.2	Forgiveness				
3.3	Non-quarrelsome				
IV	**Service**				
4.1	Helping others				
4.2	Compassion				
4.3	Dignity of Manual labour				
V	**Personal Values**				
5.1	Cleanliness				
5.2	Good Manners				
5.3	Discipline, Punctuality				
5.4	Scientific temper				
5.5	Truthfulness				
VI	**Societal Concerns**				
6.1	Preservation of Environment & Public Property				
6.2	Communal Harmony				
6.3	Aesthetic appreciation				

Signature of the Teacher

Date ______________

The students Record of Values proforma may be filled once in every quarter.

The teacher may find it difficult to fill up the proforma unless he / she keeps a record of daily happenings in the institution. It is, therefore, advisable that each teacher may maintain a Daily Diary. In this Diary, a page may be earmarked for each student. Generally specific anecdotes may be recorded in this Diary. It may not be desirable to write observations daily for each student. The Daily Diary will prove a useful for the teacher to fill up in every quarter the proforma for students 'Record of Values.'

Corrective measures may be taken by the teacher / institution whenever and wherever needed.

Overall remarks about each student may be written in students Progress Report Card at the end of the school session i. e. at the end of the third quarter.

Conclusion

The evaluation system concerning value education should foster developing of a positive self-concept in each student. Evaluation procedure must recognize the right of the child to be appreciated for what he / she is, for what he / she has the potential to become.

IX

Human Rights Education

Meaning and Importance of Human Rights

The concept of human rights derives its inspiration from the Declaration of Independence of July 4, 1776. It declared, "We hold that these truths to be self-evident that all men are created equal, that they are endowed by their creator with certain unalienable rights, that among these are life, liberty and the pursuit of happiness." So thereafter, the French Revolution of 1789 also proclaimed the slogan of "Liberty, Equality and Fraternity". But the concept of human rights as it stands today finds its international recognition in the UN Universal Declaration of Human Rights (December 10, 1948).

December 10 is celebrated as Human Rights Day.

With a view to understand the concept of human rights, it is very essential to go through the Preamble to the Universal Declaration of Human Rights.

The Preamble to the Universal Declaration of Human Rights [December 10, 1948]

Whereas recognition of the inherent dignity and of the equal and inalienable rights of all members of the human family is the foundation of freedom, justice and peace in the world.

Whereas disregard and contempt for human rights have resulted in barbarous acts which have outraged the

---

* The author is indebted to Mr. J.C. Aggarwal for his valuable contribution in this chapter.

conscience of mankind, and the advent of a world in which human beings shall enjoy freedom of speech and belief and freedom from fear and want has been proclaimed as the highest aspiration of the common people.

Whereas it is essential, if man is not to be compelled to have recourse, as a last resort, to rebellion against tyranny and oppression, that human rights should be protected by the rule of law.

Whereas it is essential, to promote the development of friendly relations between nations.

Whereas the peoples of the United Nations have in the Charter reaffirmed their faith in fundamental human rights, in the dignity and worth of the human person and in the equal rights of men and women and have determined to promote social progress and better standards of life in larger freedom.

Whereas Member States have pledged themselves to achieve, in co-operation with the United Nations, the promotion of universal respect for and observance of human rights and fundamental freedoms.

Whereas a common understanding of these rights and freedom is of the greater importance for the full realization of this pledge. Therefore the General Assembly proclaims this Universal Declaration of Human Rights :

As a common standard of achievement for all peoples and all nations, to the end that every individual and every organ of society, keeping this Declaration constantly in mind, shall strive by teaching and education to promote respect for these rights and freedoms and by progressive measures, national and international, to secure their universal and effective recognition and observance, both among the peoples of Members States themselves and among the peoples of territories under their jurisdiction.

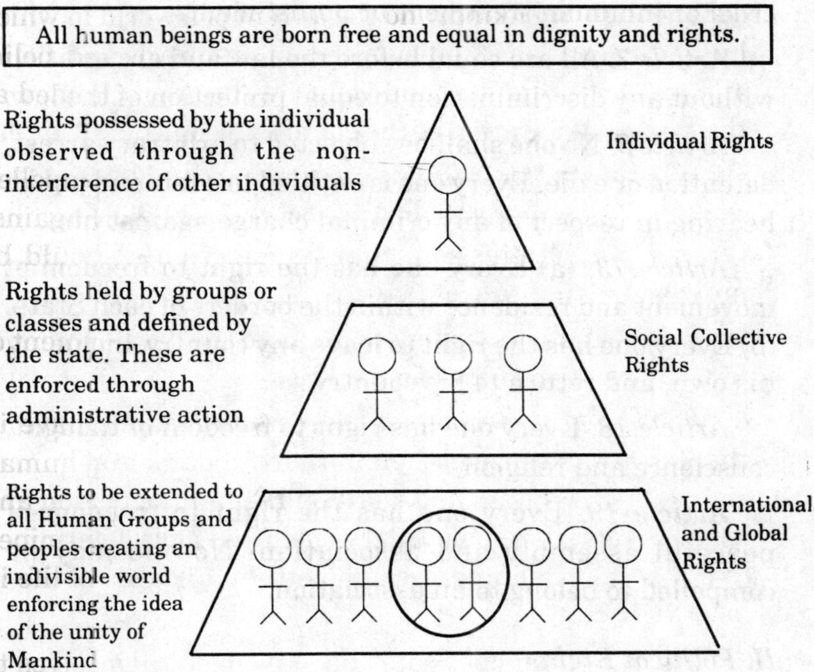

Fig. 1 : A Holistic View of Human Rights

Broad Classification of Human Rights

Thirty Articles containing in the Declaration may be grouped under the following five heads :

I. Civil Rights

Article 1. All human beings are born free and equal in dignity and rights.

Article 3. Every one has the right to life, liberty and security of person.

Article 4. No one shall be held in slavery or servitude. Slavery and the slave trade shall be prohibited in all their forms.

Article 5. No one shall be subjected to torture or to

cruel or inhuman treatment or punishment.

Article 7. All are equal before the law and are entitled without any discrimination to equal protection of the law.

Article 9. No one shall be subjected to arbitrary arrest, detention or exile. Every one is entitled to a fair and public hearing in respect of any criminal charge against him.

Article 13. (a) Every one has the right to freedom of movement and residence within the borders of each State. (b) Every one has the right to leave any country, including his own, and return to his country.

Article 18. Every one has right to freedom of thought, conscience and religion.

Article 19. Every one has the right to freedom of peaceful assembly and association. No one may be compelled to belong to an association.

II. Political Rights

These rights are as follows :

Article 21. (1) Every one has the right to take part in the government of his country, directly or though freely chosen representatives.

(2) Every one has the right of equal access to public services in his country.

(3) The 'Will of the People' shall be the basis of the authority of government. This 'Will' shall be expressed through periodic elections based on universals and equal suffrage. The elections shall be held by secret vote.

Article 15 (c). Every one has the right to a nationality. No one shall be arbitrarily deprived of his nationality. Nor shall one be denied the right to change his nationality.

Article 14. Every one has the right to seek and to enjoy in other countries asylum from persecution.

III. Economic Rights

These are as follows :

Article 17. (1) Every one has right to own property alone as well as in association with others. No one shall be arbitrarily deprived of his property.

(2) Every one has the right to social security. Social security is a system by which the government pays money regularly to people who have no other income or only a very small income.

Article 23. (1) Every one has the right to work and to protection against unemployment.

Article 23. (2) Every one has the right to equal pay for equal work.

Article 23. (3) Every one has the right to form and join trade unions for the protection of his interests.

Article 25. Every one has the right to a standard of living adequate for the health and well-being of himself and of his family. This includes proper food, clothing, housing, medical care and necessary social services.

Article 24. Every one has the right to rest and leisure, including reasonable hours of work and paid holidays.

IV. Social Rights

The social rights mentioned in the Declaration are as follows :

Article 16 (1). Men and women of full age have the right to marry and to found a family.

Article 16 (2). Marriage shall be entered into with full consent of the intending spouses.

Article 16 (3). The family is the natural and fundamental unit of society. It is entitled to full protection by society and the State.

Article 25 (2). Motherhood and childhood are entitled to special care and assistance.

Article 26 (1). Every one has the right to education. Education shall be free, at least in the elementary and fundamental stages.

Article 26 (2). The education shall promote understanding, tolerance and friendship among all nations and racial groups. It shall further the activities of the United Nations for the maintenance of peace.

V. Cultural Rights

The cultural rights of all human beings are as follows:

Article 27. (1) Every one has the right freely to participate in the cultural life of the community. In other words, every one has the right to enjoy the arts and to share in scientific advancement and its benefits.

(2) Every one has the right to the protection of the moral and material interests resulting from any scientific, literacy or artistic production of which he is the author.

Constitution of India and Human Rights

Our Constitution incorporates the major ideas of the Declaration of Human Rights through Directive Principles of State Policy and the provision of Fundamental Rights which can be enforced through law courts.

Article 14 of the Constitution provides : "The state shall not deny to any person equality before law." This provision reflects the spirit of Article 2 of the UN Declaration of Human Rights. Article 19 of our Constitution gives every Indian the right to move freely, settle and reside in any part of India. This is commensurate with the Declaration which provides for freedom of movement and residence.

Other provisions in our Constitution which are parallel to the Declaration of Human Rights include Right of Freedom of Worship and Propagation of Religion (Article 25), Right of Conservation of One's Language and Culture (Article 29); Right of Equal pay for Equal Work for both Men and Women (Article 39) and Right to have Free and Compulsory Education up to the age of 14 (Article 45).

Constitution of India : Fundamental Rights similar to the UN Human Rights

1. Right to Equality before the Law (Article 14)
2. Freedom from Discrimination (Article 15)
3. Right to Equal Opportunity in Public Employment (Article 16)
4. Right to Freedom of Speech and Expression (Article 19)
5. Right to Assemble Peacefully without Arms (Article 19)
6. Right to form Associations or Unions (Article 19)
7. Right to Move Freely (Article 19)
8. Right to Settle and Reside Anywhere in the Country (Article 19)
9. Right to Practise any Profession, Occupation, Trade Business (Article 19)
10. Right Not to be convicted of Offences Not Crimes at Time Committed (Article 20)
11. Right to Life and Personal Liberty (Article 21)
12. Right not to be Detained Without Being Informed of Reasons (Article 22)
13. Right to Consult with, and be Defended by a Lawyer After Arrest (Article 22)
14. Right Against Trafficking in Human Beings and Forced Labour (Article 23)

15. Right Against Employment of Children (under 14 years) in Factories, Mines or Dangerous Jobs (Article 24)
16. Right to Freedom of Conscience and Freedom of Religion (Article 25-28)
17. Right to Protection of Cultural Rights of Minorities (Article 29)
18. Right to Protection of Educational Rights of Minorities (Article 30)
19. Right to Approach the Supreme Court if Rights Violated (Article 31).

Education for Human Rights, Cooperation and Non-Violence

Education has been specified as one of the fundamental human rights vide Article 26 of the 'Universal Declaration of Human Rights' follows :

Article 26 (i) "Everyone has the right to education. Education shall be free, at least in the elementary and fundamental stages. Technical and professional education shall be equally accessible to all on the basis of merit."

(ii) "Education shall be directed to the full development of the human personality and to the strengthening of respect for human rights and fundamental freedoms."

It shall promote understanding, tolerance and friendship among all nation, racial or religious groups and shall further the activities of the United Nations for the maintenance of peace."

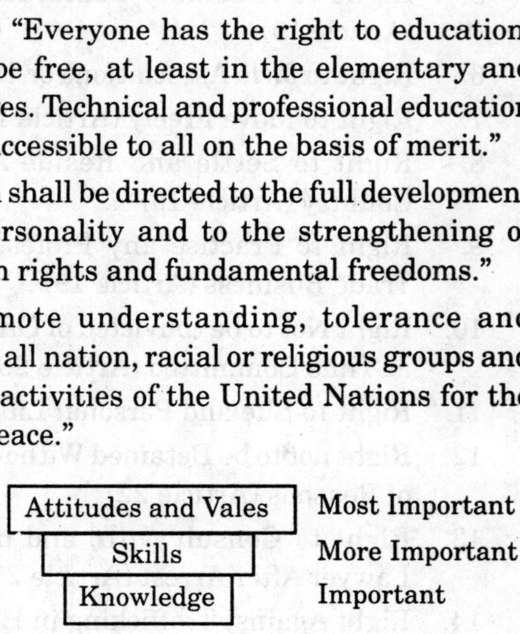

Fig. 2 : Hierarchy of Objectives of Human Rights Education

(iii) "Parents have a prior right to choose the kind of education that shall be given to their children.

Thus, being a human right, education has essentially 'to contribute to the development of global human rights culture'. This is why all human rights documents have stressed the need for education in human rights at all important stages namely policy formulation, curriculum development and actual teaching-learning activities.

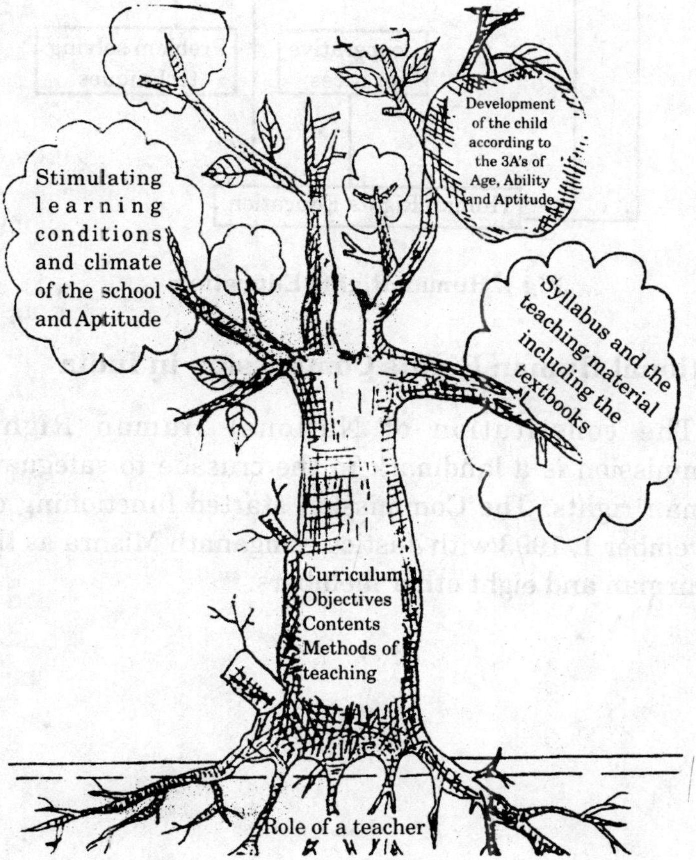

Fig. 3 : A Overall View - a theoretical framework of Human Rights teaching

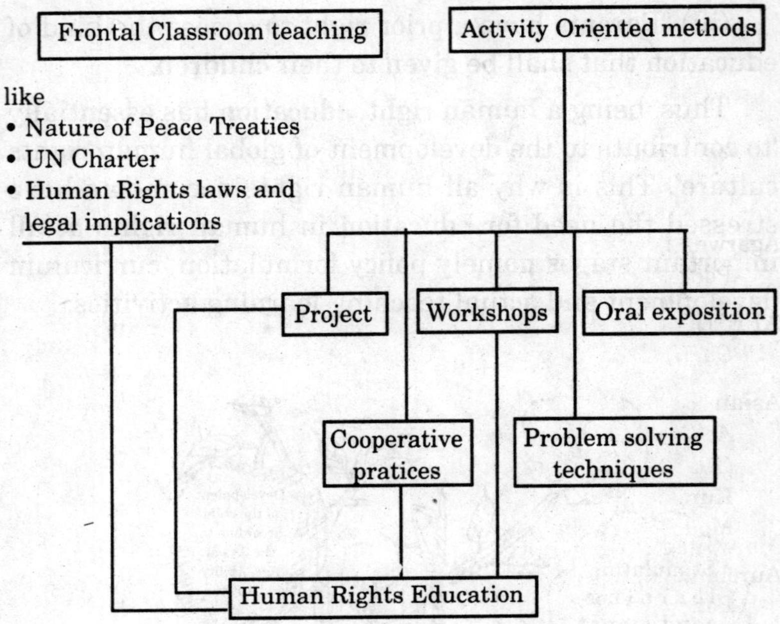

Fig 4. Human Rights Education

National Human Rights Commission in India

The constitution of National Human Rights Commission is a landmark in the crusade to safeguard human rights. The Commission started functioning on November 1, 1993 with Justice Ranganath Mishra as the Chairman and eight other members.

Bibliography

Agarwal, Arun K. (1998), Developing Self Confidence, New Delhi; Hind Pocket Books.

APEID, *Values and Ethics and the Science and Technology Curriculum*, Bangkok, UNESCO, 1991.

Asian Educationists Conference in *Human Rights and Values, Achieving the Goals of UN Decade for Human Rights Education (1995-2004)*, June 22 to 25, 1997 organised by Prajapati Brahma Kumaris Ishwariya Vishwavidyalaya International Headquarters, Mount Abu, *Education in Asia* 17(2), 1997, pp. 142-144.

Aurobindo, *System of National Education: Some Preliminary Ideas*. Pondicherry, Sri Aurobindo Ashram, 1970.

Baba, S.S.S., Spiritual Basis of Value Education, *Santhana Sarathi*, October 1977, pp. 269-272.

Bantock, G.H., *Education and Values : Essays in the Theory of Education*, London, Faber and Faber, 1967.

Beck John, *Morality and Citizenship in Education*, London, Willington House, 1998.

Billing, J.C., Teaching Values by Example, *Illinois School Board Journal*, 58, 1990 pp. 28-29.

Budhanada Swami, *How to Build Character : A Primer* New Delhi, Ramakrishna Mission, 1983

Buzzelu, C.A., Young Children's Moral Understanding: Learning about Right and Wrong, *Young Children*, 47(6), 1992, pp. 47-53.

Cairn, S Jo; Lawton, Denis; Gardner, Roy, Eds. *Value, Culture and Education : World Year Book on Education, 2001* London, Kogan Page, 2001.

Carr, D., Moral Values and the Teacher : Beyond the Paternal and the Permissive, *Journal of Philosophy of Education*, 27, 1993, pp. 193-207.

Central Board of Secondary Education, Value Education : a Handbook for Teachers, New Delhi, the author, 1997

Chittibabu, S.V., Value-orientation in Higher Education, *Progressive Educational Herald* 2(2), 1988.

Choudhary, K. (1996), Value Education in India; The Socio-ideological Dimensions. Indian Journal of Social Research, Vol.37(i), p.15-26.

Cragg, A.W., Moral education in the school: The Hidden Values Argument, *Interchange*. 10, (1), 1978. pp. 12-19.

Cummings, Rhoda; Harlow, Steve, Constructivist Roots of Moral Education, *The Educational Forum*. 64; (4), 2000. pp. 300-307.

Das, R.C., Study of the methods adopted by selected Secondary Schools in India for development of moral and ethical values and measurement of value judgment of students of class IX of these schools, Bhubaneswar, Regional College of Education, 1991.

Dave, Indu, Concept of Value Education, *Rajasthan Board Journal of Education*, 27, (23), 1991, pp.1-6.

DeRoche, Edward F; Williams, Mary M., Educating Hearts and Minds : Comprehensive Character Education Framework. California, Corwin Press, 1998, Development. Early Education and Development; Special issue on : *Early Education for Moral Development* 11(1) Jan 2000.

Dhar, P.L., How can Values be Taught? *Journal of Value Education*, November 2000.

Ediger Marlow, Values and Curriculum, *New Frontiers in Education* 12(3), 1982.

Education for Values Development, Chapter 5. In National Curriculum Framework for School Education, New Delhi, NCERT, 2000, pp. 117-119.

Edwars, J; Pogelman, K, *Developing Citizenship in the Curriculum*, London, Fulton, 1993.

Erricker, Clive; Erricker, Jane, *Reconstructing Religious, Spiritual and Moral Education*. New York, Routledge Falmer, 2000.

Gaikwad Shashi, Role of Women in Education for Human Rights and Values, *Education in Asia* 17(2), 1997, pp. 128-129.

Ginsberg Morris, *Swami Vivekananda on Universal Ethics and Moral Conduct India*, Ministry of Education, 1965.

Halstead, J.M. and M.J. Tayler, *Values and Values Education in Schools, In values in Education and Education in Values*, ed., by London, Falmer Press, 1996

Halstead, J.M. and M.J. Tayler, *Liberal Values and Liberal Education, In Values in Education and Education in Values*, ed. by London, Falmer Press, 1996.

Heaman, John, *Cornerstone Values – a Value Education Curriculum*, New Zealand Foundation for Values Education, 1996.

Jorrett James L, *The Teaching of Values : Caring and Appreciation*, London, Routledge, 1991.

Joshi, Kireet, Education for Personality Development, New Delhi, NCERT, 1976, (NIE Lecture Series).

Kaila, H. L. & Kushal (1998), Parents and Value Education, Mumbai; D.A.V. Centre for Creative Education.

Kalra, R.M., *Teaching of Science with Focus on Values*, New Delhi : Vikas Publishers. 2002.

Kalra, R.M., *Curriculum Development with a Focus on Values*. Ambala: International Book Agencies, 1977.

Kalra, R. M. (2002), Value Oriented Education in Schools, New Delhi; Shipra Publications.

Kishore Lalit, *Value Oriented Education : Foundation and Frontiers – World Overview*, Delhi, Doaba House, 1990.

Kluckhohn, C, *Values and Values Orientation in the Theory of Action: An exploration in definition and classification. In towards a general theory of social action*, ed. by T. Parson and E.A. Shill, Cambridge, Harvard University Press, 1951.

Linda and Richard Eyre (1995), Teaching your Children Values, (Teaching your children sensitivity), New York, Rockefeller Center.

Nanda R.T., *Contemporary approaches to Value Education in India*, New Delhi, Regency, 1997.

National Council for Teacher Education, *Human Rights and National Values : Self-learning Modules for Teacher Education*, New Delhi, the author, 1999.

Passi B.K., *Value Education*, Agra, National Psychological Press, 1991.

Poole, M., *Beliefs and Values in Science Education*, Buckingham, Open University Press, 1995.

Paul W. Tayler, *Respect for Nature*, Princeton University Press, Princeton, New Jersey, USA, 1994.

Raths, L. Harmin, M.; Simon, S. *Values and Teaching: Working with Values in the Classroom*, Columbus OH, Merril, 1996.

Radhakrishna, S., *Religion and Society*, London, George Allen and Unwin, 1959.

Riley, Sue Spayth, *How to Generate Values in Young Children*, Washington, National Association for the Education of Young Children, 1989.

Rowe, D. Newton, J. eds., *You, Me, Us : A new Approach to moral and Social Education for Primary Schools*. London, Citizenship Foundation, 1994.

Ruhela, S.P., *Human Values and Education*, New Delhi, Sterling Publication, 1986.

Ruhela, S.P. (1996) Education in Human Values, New Delhi; Regency Publication.

Sharma, O.P., *Value Education in Action*, Jaipur, University Book House, 1997.

Shrimali, K.L., *Search for Value in Indian Education*, Delhi, Vikas, 1971.

Simon, S.B. Howe, I.W.; Kirschenbaum. H., *Values Clarification: a Handbook of Practical Strategies for Teachers and Students*, New York, Hart Publishing, 1972.

Swami Vivekananda : Complete Work, Calcutta, Advaita Ashram, 1992, Vol. I, pp. 389.

Symonds, P.M. (1964), What Education has to learn from Psychology, New York; Teacher's College, Columbia University.

Taylor, M.J. ed., *Values Education in Europe*: a comparative overview of a survey of 26 countries in 1993 Dundee, SCCC for UNESCO/ CIDREE, 1994, Teacher Training Authority, 1997.

Thomas Lickona, Education for Character : The school's highest calling, Georgia Humanities Council, 199 (Lecture)

Thomas Lickona, *Education for Character – How our schools can teach respect and responsibility*, Bantam Books, 1992.

Vedarajan, P, *Teaching Human Values through Co-curriculum Activities*. In education for human excellence, Delhi, CBSE, 2000.

Walia, K., Value based teacher education views of modern Indian thinkers. *Journal of Values Education*, November, 2000.

West, Sylvia, *Educational Values for School Leadership*, London, Kogan Page, 1993.

World Health Organization (1997) Young People and their Families; A Cross Cultural Study of Parent/ Adolescent Discord in Cote d'Ivoire, India and Nigeria, Geneva, Switzerland.

